ENGAGING GUYANA'S DIASPORA WITH THE FIERCE URGENCY OF NOW!

Dr. Michael Ralph Sr.

DEDICATION

This book is dedicated to my wife Lynette, and to my sons Wole, Michael and Laurence. My heartfelt thanks go to each of them for their support and encouragement.

CONTENTS

The Fierce Urgency of Now (FUN) Blueprint for Diaspora Engagement

ACKNOWLEDGMENTS

I gratefully acknowledge and express deep appreciation to the many wonderful people who have made this book possible. To my parents whose lives and teachings reflected the wisdom of the ages, I assure you that I have learned from your legacy. To my university colleagues, and students, your sharing, knowledge and synergy have moved me levels beyond my own thinking. To my wife, I thank you for your patience, insight, and guidance on bibliographic formatting. To my son Laurence and his other half Aisha - the two Harvard professors, I thank you for your useful insights during our discussion last Christmas, when this project was in its infancy.

1 FUN BLUEPRINT

Diaspora Engagement – A Call to Action

First, a word about the context and title of this book is necessary. It was in April 1967, just a year before he was assassinated that Rev. Martin Luther King Jr. preached a sermon titled the "Fierce Urgency of Now." King called for Christians to break their silence about the atrocities uncovered during the war in Vietnam and join in the struggle for human rights and world peace. Many US citizens and other peace-loving supporters around the world joined in the struggle for equal rights, human rights and world peace. This current "Call for Action" to the Guyanese Diaspora is motivated from a different context. The latter is context of the urgent need for affirmative or positive action to address and foster Guyana's national development.

It prevails on all Guyanese, particularly those in the diaspora to rise to the challenge of "The Fierce Urgency of Now!" to participate in the development efforts of their country. In this context, two questions may be raised, "If not now, when?" and "If not you, then who?"

The uniqueness of this book derives from the fact that it does not merely provide information that the reader is expected to learn or memorize. It is meant to stimulate action! It is A Call to Action! - An appeal to all in the Guyanese diaspora, and others living in Guyana to summon their national affinity and civic pride for the Homeland and contribute to the continued development to their nation from wherever they reside.

Whether individually, in family groups, in clubs or associations, or as a task force, any group interested in developmental activities can use this model to structure, track and assess their activities with meticulous determination to ensure tasks that are completed in a sequential manner toward goal attainment. Before proceeding further however, it is essential to define some important terms and concepts for clarification.

According to the Merriam Webster dictionary the meaning of the word "Blueprint" is originally a photographic print in white on a bright blue background, used primarily as a guide for erecting buildings, structures and machinery. However, this meaning has expanded in contemporary usage to encompass other configurations and to serve as an illustrated model or guidance for using a series of steps to erect a physical or theoretical structure.

In short, a "Blueprint" illustrates a mode for making, doing or accomplishing something of value. Following this expanded use, the word is used figuratively in this book to mean a model for providing guidance, a plan, or schema toward the worthwhile important goals of engagement in national development.

This Blueprint for Diaspora Engagement is a structured, yet flexible methodology for the engagement of the Guyanese diaspora in national development. It illustrates a strategic approach with built-in sequences for revising and updating the original schema with new data and information as the engagement process unfolds.

In this manner, the results of these actions are constantly recycled into a continuous revisionary and improvement process to strengthen the blueprint.

This book represents logical sequential steps to stimulate thinking and action by the users, while making it clear that these steps may be adjusted as the metrics of the development activities change. At each stage the experiential actions need to be assessed and sequenced back thus increasing the viability of the model (as explained earlier). Diaspora engagement can be expected to differ by variables such as ethnic culture, language and the social-economic and political dynamics of diaspora members. In every instance though, participants are directed to ideals such as the improvement of the status quo in the targeted national arena.

The meaning of the word "Diaspora"

According to the Webster's and Oxford dictionaries, the word "diaspora" derives from the Greek language, and means a scattering or dispersion. It refers to a scattered population group to larger geographic regions with origins within a smaller geographic location. The term diaspora is in addition the movement of a specific population from its ancestral land or the land of its birth.

Examples of historical Diasporas include the forcible expulsion of the Jews from Judea, the exodus of Greeks after the fall of Constantinople, and the African Trans-Atlantic slave trade. At the time of writing, the world is witnessing the spread of another diaspora as citizens of war-torn Syria are leaving their homeland to seek asylum in other countries willing to accept them. Urged by United Nations' appeals, countries throughout the globe are processing applications for settling Syrian refugees. These countries include the United States, Canada, the United Kingdom, others in the Middle East, countries scattered all across Europe and others in every corner of the globe.

Researchers and scholars have often postulated that Diasporas may be divided into different types by their causes such as whether these were originated by imperialism, labor migrations, weather catastrophes, war or other means. Regardless of their origin or typology, many diaspora members have established and maintained strong ties with the homeland. Occasionally, they may travel back for familial and national events. Many maintain societal and political linkage with their homeland and may eventually choose permanent residence. In this respect, the Guyanese diaspora is no different. It was created from national, political and economic strife and the struggle for better educational and other social opportunities.

As with other Diasporas, after the crisis that prompted members to leave their homeland has abated, the homeland can become a major magnet for diaspora members. Often it serves as a target for foreign direct investment (FDI) for diaspora investors, technology transfer, philanthropy, tourism, political contributions, and intangible flows of knowledge, new attitudes, and cultural influences. So far, the concentrated and impenetrable web of links between Guyana as its diaspora is, in the overwhelming majority of cases, the creation of individuals and groups acting on their own initiative, irrespective of initiatives of from the leaders of the nation.

The blueprint unveiled here, has the potential to bring individuals and groups together who desire to be engaged in national development. Typical groups may comprise family and extended family members, organizational members, ethnic or other affinity members, alumni cohorts, religious members and sundry groups of every kind. Typically some comprise members of professional associations, charitable organizations, development NGOs, investment group members, affiliates of political parties, humanitarian relief organizations, schools and clubs for the preservation of culture, virtual networks, and federations of associations.

Diaspora members may make their contributions through these organizations, and use their group strengths and dynamics to make the climate more conducive for stimulating effective national development. Thousands of Guyanese migrants from diaspora populations have strong roots in their country of origin and want to assist in any way they can with national development commensurate with their knowledge, skills and capabilities. Their linguistic, cultural familiarity and outreach to national partners can be potentially effective and successful in assisting to make developmental projects successful. This is a very positive phenomena, but one that needs to be harnessed and utilized to the best interest of the homeland.

With respect to the current state of affairs in Guyana, diaspora volunteers can help to counter the effects of the "talent drain or brain drain" experienced by the nation, as they become more active participants in national developmental initiatives.

The Guyana Diaspora has emerged as a potentially major developmental actor in an increasingly interdependent global arena. It is now widely comprised of persons of multiple professions and occupational categories – teachers, nurses, doctors, university professors, business owners and corporate leaders, financiers, bankers, investors, engineers, computer science specialists, scientists, international leaders, multi-talented affinity groups, and others. Some in the Guyanese diaspora have accumulated a variety of critical resources, social and financial capital and other strengths that are useful for making significant contributions to the political and socio-economic development of Guyana.

Additionally, many others are employed in high skill sectors that are of critical importance to Guyana's developmental aspirations. Many of these diaspora members have acquired requisite entrepreneurial ability and knowledge, both of which are needed for the successful establishment and management of new local and international business enterprises. A significant number have relationships and contacts with business partners and potential investors in the US, Canada and the UK, European and other countries. These actors are capable of assisting in facilitating investment in trade and, in large, medium and smaller production enterprises as well. Some operate in influential, societal positions that have become critical for engendering positive socio-economic and political outcomes in Guyana.

Diaspora members have a unique psychological connection to their homeland. This helps them to establish and sustain connections and involvement in their home country as noted by researchers like (Safran 1991).[1] It is in acknowledgement of this fact that some developing countries have passed laws to offer dual citizenship and encourage continuous relationships with diaspora members.

This book provides a sequential approach to stakeholder diaspora engagement, beginning with empirical research, needs assessments, data collection and analysis.

The survey of diaspora skills, capabilities and professions is an important component and starting point of the blueprint, because the needs assessments and survey instruments assist in the accumulation of a solid database for decision-making. These are important for mapping stakeholders by their skills, occupations and capabilities; thus serving as a repository of a manpower talent pool available for engagement in the painstaking work of development.

---

[1] Safran W (1991) Diasporas in modern societies: Myths of homeland and return. Diaspora 1

[2] Lessinger, J., Investing or Going Home? A Transnational Strategy among Indian Immigrants in the United States, Academy of Sciences, 1992, pp. 53-80. & Guarnizo, L.E. and Smith, M.P., (1998) 'The Locations of Transnationalism 1998, pp. 3-34.

An initial task is to accumulate and use the responses from the needs assessment and survey to classify and prioritize diaspora stakeholders using metrics such as their skills, knowledge, specializations, interests, willingness, and readiness to participate.

Diaspora engagement with FUN

The acronym FUN has a dual meaning. The most obvious is that it is an abbreviation for the Fierce Urgency of Now, and urges immediate action. However, it embodies an alternate psychological concept as well.

The latter emerges from a deep conviction that diaspora engagement needs to be FUN and reflect the intrinsic joy diaspora volunteers experience from engagement in the purposeful and fulfilling work of contributing to the development of their homeland. The environment for engagement encompasses the emotive and spiritual component for national development; namely that sense of patriotism, national affinity, civic pride and fulfillment that naturally fuels the efforts of diaspora members engaged in effective, meaningful development.

It answers that important question of why does this matter? why should I be engaged in the work of national development? On an existential level, one needs to be involved when the work of development is in alignment with one's innate creative strengths, or with those gifts and talents that spark genuine interest, passion, and motivation. This capability is different from things for which one has a special talent, but may not enjoy doing. Joyful engagement, or engagement with FUN, does not mean that volunteers should feel carefree about their development tasks; but instead, have positive feelings on a consistent basis about their tasks, and are intrinsically motivated to "go the extra mile" to complete them. In this way not only are they empowered in their engagement, but also fully using their talents and potential. This emotive capacity to their involvement generates positive outcomes for both the individual and the diaspora engagement enterprise.

Critical strategic components of the FUN Blueprint

This strategic approach to engagement begins with empirical data garnered from an initial comprehensive needs assessment survey of diaspora skills. The needs assessment survey will identify:

a) Diaspora knowledge and abilities, occupational and professional skills

b) Data for conducting, a situational inventory, environmental scan foresight analysis, and issue analysis;

c) Information for formulating an engagement vision, mission, philosophy, goals, objectives, strategies, action-plans, resource allocation, assessment, accountability and feedback for the engagement enterprise and processes. These components are outlined below.

This FUN Blueprint for engagement is a tool for the application of a structured, yet flexible methodology for the engagement of the Guyanese diaspora in national development. It illuminates a strategic approach that is dynamic, as it is constantly updated with new data and information as the engagement process unfolds. As the engagement operations and goals set in advance are achieved, they will become milestones attained and an integral part of the "FUN Blueprint" or model.

The 'Call' for the principle of urgency, or "the Fierce Urgency of Now", demands that priorities be determined and quickly addressed to create an essential development momentum, rather than suffer an endless "paralysis of analysis" that has characterized earlier development initiatives in Guyana.

It urges establishing clear priorities based on what is desirable in the present and future. Then, by acting on priorities quickly, the effort needs to be directed to utilizing the resources on hand immediately while the search for complementary resources ensues.

The principle of thoughtful expediency, or 'results, instead of endless studies' is encouraged. Lessons from the past have shown that never-ending debates about ideology, political rights, legal principles, administrative procedures, and precepts can easily become impediments to the goal of improving the material living conditions of as many people as possible, as quickly as possible. Delays in implementing a forward developmental thrust needs to be avoided. Development projects and initiatives need to be considered clear and present national priorities.

The Call to Action recommends swift logical steps to stimulate thinking and action while strategies are adjusted as the metrics for development changes. As early experiential development actions are taken, assessed and fed back into the model, high standards can be maintained. Diaspora engagement can be expected to differ by the diaspora groups involved and the priorities identified. Generally though, in spite of the location of the diaspora resident or group, their commitment to national development is desirable.

Thousands of Guyanese migrants comprising the diaspora have strong roots in their country of origin and want to know what they can do to help. They desire to rely on their professional expertise, knowledge, skills, and technical assistance to aid national development efforts. With their linguistic and cultural familiarity, that engagement can be effective and more successful than efforts that have in the past omitted them from national development efforts. Diaspora volunteers can help to counter the effects of the lack of qualified specialists that has become an all too familiar consequence of Guyanese migration abroad.

Voluntary national development programs have the promise of engaging volunteers and utilizing their perspectives as they engage in developmental projects for Guyana. The Guyana diaspora has become an available resource and a potentially major developmental actor in an increasingly interdependent global arena. It is now widely acknowledged that as international leaders, groups and communities, Guyanese living overseas have accumulated financial resources, and represent human and social capital that are capable of making significant contributions to the political and socio-economic development of Guyana.

Additionally, many in the diaspora are employed in technical, medical, financial, educational and technological high skill sectors that are of critical importance to the continued development of Guyana. Others have acquired much needed entrepreneurial ability and knowledge, desperately needed for the successful establishment and management of a variety of Guyanese business enterprises. Many have relationships and contacts with business partners and potential investors in the US, Canada and the UK and other countries and are capable of assisting in facilitating investment in trade, manufacturing enterprises and in small and medium-sized companies.

A number are in influential positions in the countries where they have settled and hold societal positions critical for engendering

positive socio-economic and political transnational and multinational relationships potentially beneficial to Guyana. Swift action is needed for an injection of these much-needed manpower resources as partners, ready with a commitment to act, rebuild trust between diaspora and homeland parties, and create a much more favorable context for a national development. Of fundamental importance is the capitalization of the skills and expertise of this group to support national development efforts as soon as possible.

2 THE DIASPORA INTERNATIONAL CENTER FOR ENGAGEMENT (DICE)

The Diaspora International Center for Engagement (DICE) is a 501(c) 3 non-profit organization founded in 2016 to focus on issues between the Guyanese Diaspora and the homeland of Guyana. DICE is a nonprofit capacity-building Center and resource organization for mission-driven homeland development enterprises, processes, and initiatives.

It collaborates with government, corporate, and diaspora leaders to help scale, impact, build leadership, advance philanthropic effectiveness, and accelerate national development.

Being dedicated to issues related to Guyana's most important challenges, its focus is on breaking cycles of intergenerational poverty, providing effective safety nets, and ensuring core human and civil rights. Its services include strategy consulting, capacity-building, project initiation, leadership development, philanthropic advising, and skills training and developing and sharing practical insights.

Vision, Mission Statement and Values

The Diaspora International Center for Engagement's (DICE) vision is a diaspora actively engaged in homeland development projects and initiatives. This work would extend across the globe, creating an enabling environment that is essential for Guyana to flourish economically, socially, politically and culturally, embracing expected regional and global trends of the world of today and tomorrow.

Mission Statement

DICE is dedicated to building better relationships between the Guyanese Diaspora and the homeland through the engagement of the diaspora in supporting and contributing to national development planning, processes, initiatives and projects.

DICE's Values

The Center's values are

- *Respect:* We listen to and learn from governmental representatives, Guyanese nationals, diaspora residents, funders, and those concerned and grounded in its mission

- *Impact:* We value performance and results. We set and hold ourselves accountable for high standards about the national interests of Guyana. We value diverse perspectives and the transference of knowledge

- *Candor:* Good choices are grounded in empirical data and information. We value facts and feedback, speak our minds, and understand that hard choices, logical and difficult tradeoffs are often necessary

- *Collaboration:* We work as a team within DICE, with the diaspora and citizens of Guyana. We share what we know and try to align our efforts with those of others who are dedicated to achieving economic, social and political developmental impact for Guyana

- *Passion:* We are committed to making a difference through purposeful and fulfilling work. DICE values all diaspora contributions to the development of the homeland of Guyana as they strive for sustainability in national development

Date of Founding:

Who does DICE Serve?

DICE is as an international membership organization made up of Guyanese diaspora members, all other Guyanese citizens and their advocates.

DICE *Programs and Services*

DICE chooses to accomplish its mission in a number of ways:

- Advocacy for international and local engagement;

- Fundraising and grant writing to raise funding for center operations and programs;

- Funding awards in the form of mini-grants Guyana development projects

- Implementation of larger scale national development projects; Annual & periodic Conferences and meetings in diaspora development engagement issues and perspectives;

- Inviting scholarly papers on implementing national development projects in Guyana for national technological improvement, development of alternate sources of energy (solar, hydro-electric, wind, wave) and others of wide-scale infrastructure transformation;

- Training and skill building for diaspora members, volunteers and leaders engaged in national development;

- Public policy development education and project engagement;

- Initiation and improvement of local manufacturing industries;

- Establishing university exchange, research and cooperative partnerships for learning and teaching

Projects & Goals

The goals of the Center are to:

2. Procure grant and other sponsorship funding for development projects and initiatives.

3. Conduct annual and periodic fund raising projects and activities to leverage funding for development initiatives,

4. Fund and strengthen the financial sustainability of development initiatives and projects,

5. Strengthen the relationships among members and increase their knowledge, effectiveness and capacity for collective action,

6. Strengthen the relationships between diaspora members and Guyana development actors and increase the knowledge, effectiveness and capacity for collective action of both groups,

7. Build bridges between diaspora members and key Guyanese institutions (business, local government, philanthropic and others) to increase partnership and cooperation,

8. Increase opportunities for the implementation of development programs, shared services and opportunities for capacity building,

9. Implement urgently needed priority development projects,

10. Initiate a student internship for graduate students in the discipline of international development.

3 DESCRIPTION OF THE FUN BLUEPRINT

The main visual feature of the blueprint is a triangle within a circle (as illustrated below). The component phases of the blueprint, as represented in the triangle, move upward from a broad base to an increasingly narrower focus.

The broadest focus is the all encompassing *Vision,* or desired future, representing development of the nation at the highest level, when the Blueprint is used as a guide for national development. Alternately, the Blueprint may be used to guide initiatives or projects at a lower level of organization.

Next, as we move upward, are *Philosophy & Mission and Goals.* Likewise, these focuses may apply at the highest level to the nation as a whole or at lower levels to narrower initiatives. A similar pattern applies to other focuses like objectives, strategies, action plans and accountability. These sequential phases are intended to apply to all development initiatives whether they are national level projects, or at lower level, sectorial, initiatives and projects.

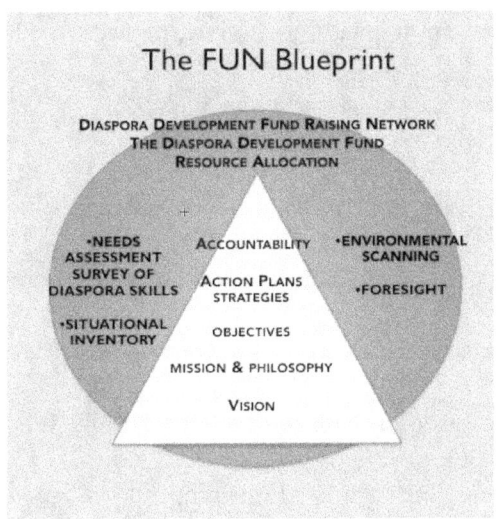

Within the circle, are other important entities; namely a Diaspora Engagement Network (DEN), and a Diaspora International Fund. Additionally, on the sides of the triangle are internal and external assessments, aided by an initial survey and needs assessment of diaspora skills, professions and interests, a situational inventory, a continuous environmental scanning process and foresight initiation. These sequences will provide the data and empirical information for decision making for development projects and initiatives. The blueprint is best viewed as a roadmap or guide for the implementation and progression of any typical initiative or project for development purposes when viewed comprehensively.

A circle indicates the boundaries of the Blueprint. This circle encompasses the emotive and spiritual component for national development. Namely the sense of patriotism, national affinity, civic pride and fulfillment that should fuel the efforts of diaspora members engaged meaningfully in development.

The blueprint guides strategic planning and implementation as essential components through the Internal and External Assessment phases. This assessment comprises an analysis and evaluation of internal and external data and factors that affect both priorities. It involves:

a) A Situational Inventory: This is an assessment of the diaspora group's position, performance, problems, and potential. It includes a values audit (an analysis of the group's organizational philosophy).

b) An Environmental scanning process: An analysis of key external elements or forces (national and international) that affect the environment in which the diaspora collaborative group functions.

c) Foresight: Explicit efforts to systematically identify, monitor, and analyze long-term trends and issues that are likely to affect the collaborative group's future environment and to examine the implications those trends and issues may hold for the group's future.

d) <u>Issue Analysis</u>: An identification and analysis of strategic issues—problems or concerns of critical importance to the collaborative group and its stakeholders, and expectation groups. The blueprint' planning process is inspired by a shared vision of the future. This vision, along with the diaspora's mission and philosophy, are part of the group's identity and "uniqueness." Therefore, the FUN Blueprint identifies the eight phases described earlier namely:

<u>Vision</u>: A compelling conceptual image of the desired future.

<u>Mission</u>: A broad, comprehensive statement of the group's purpose.

<u>Philosophy</u>: The organization's core values, describing how the organization conducts itself in carrying out its mission.

To answer the question "Where do we want to be?" the FUN Blueprint for strategic planning identifies:

<u>Goals</u>: The general end purposes toward which effort is directed.

Objectives: Specific, measurable targets for accomplishment. To discover "How do we get there?" strategic planning develops:

Strategies: The methods used to accomplish goals and objectives.

Action Plans: Detailed descriptions of how strategies will be implemented on an operational basis.

To determine "How do we measure our progress?" the FUN Blueprint builds in:

Accountability: The methods used to measure results. Finally, the blueprint guides:

Resource Allocation: The determination and allotment of resources necessary to carry out strategies and achieve objectives, within the priority framework established in the goal-setting process. The FUN Blueprint emphasizes the deployment of resources to achieve meaningful results. That is, the deliberate use of planning to drive budgeting.

Imperatives for implementation

Implementing diaspora collaborative group level actions occur within the following context: The group formulates their vision, policies, goals, and priorities by working in concert with national representatives assigned to this task.

FUN Blueprint and strategic action plans are formulated consistent with policies and priorities established by these two groups. Frequently, the mission of a national development program or activity undertaken by a department or agency is delineated in the enabling legislation or executive order for that activity or program. Guidelines and assumptions for programmatic planning may be provided to departments and agencies by the official administrative departments. Legislative Auditors may also provide guidelines for performance audits to departments and agencies. These stipulations and directives form the basis for needs assessments in major policy or functional areas, to be used for planning and budgeting with national and diaspora groups.

Blueprint Strategic engagement & Planning Process

The Diaspora Collaborative Group (DCG) volunteer members participate because of their commitment to devote their time, effort, and specialized expertise to development issues. Typically, the DCG can be expected to include knowledgeable individuals from various national and diaspora programs or services relative to the demands of the national development program or initiative. Many national agencies already have executive management teams that routinely meet and resolve development management issues. This group may serve as the nucleus of the planning team, along with any additional resource persons needed.

These may include, national program managers, supervisors, and others, who use detailed involvement with a program to carry the planning process into the operational program level. They define program missions, philosophies, formulate program goals and specific objectives; build strategies to achieve objectives; operationalize strategies

31

through action plans; establish and maintain accountability; and determine needed resources.

The DCG is best seen merely as a resource to assist in analyzing the overseas impacts of potential strategies, and use strategic plans to guide development of strategies to make the program or initiative understandable to overseas partners and audiences.

Funding sponsors, local and overseas banks and partners understandably use strategic plans to guide development of capital outlay plans and budgets. Thus, the diaspora planning coordinator can appropriately provide the coordination and tools for moving the initiative through the planning process.

The planning coordinator develops the timetable for planning and organizes and documents the entire process. FUN Blueprint strategy planning (BSP) coordinators are part of the diaspora network. Training for BSP coordinators should be completed prior to their assignment.

A trained experienced facilitator from the diaspora network

is needed to guide participants through planning sessions, assuring that all views are considered. This facilitator should be neutral; he or she should not express personal opinions but instead serve to keep the discussion flowing. ("Facilitator" is a functional title, not a position.) The chosen facilitator is usually someone apart from the diaspora network.

Many organizations prefer to have an outsider facilitate their planning sessions, particularly high-level ones with requisite experience from the corporate or governmental sectors. Carrying the FUN Blueprint Strategic Planning Process to the Program Level requires effective technical assistance.

"Budget unit" is a term used in budget development to designate the sub-group as the other authorized unit of the DCG. Officially, a budget unit is any spending group declared to be a budget entity by administrations. Each budget unit may be divided into programs. A program is defined as a grouping of activities that results in the accomplishment of an objective or set of objectives for each activity within the program. A program must be delineated into activities, which are program components representing distinct subsets of functions or services. Strategic planning guides resource allocation through annual operating plans and budgets as well as capital outlay plans and budgets. For operational budget development, a budget request and operational plan should be submitted for each program activity, and operational funds may be appropriated by the leadership sub-group of the program. The capital outlay planning and budgeting process requires an explanation of the program impacts of each capital project being pursued. The FUN Blueprint strategic process should be carried down to the program level within each budget unit and must include the activities for each program.

The most effective diaspora engagement programs are those initiated in response to the requests of diaspora members. These include diaspora volunteer engagement initiatives, networking alliances, technical assistance programs and other associated enterprises.

4 HISTORICAL IMPERATIVES

Though rich in natural resources, Guyana has struggled for decades with the problems of politico-economic-cultural and racial tensions. These struggles ensued against a backdrop of political upheaval that has long conditioned the nature of these challenges. However, at this point, in its existence and development, the country is poised either to leave its racial divisiveness behind and go forward with hope for a more brilliant and hopeful future or to remain mired in the struggles of the past.

Though Guyana is marked by ethnic differences between two nearly equivalent major population groups;

there has not been as much ethnic violence in Guyana, compared to other hotspots globally where ethnic strife has fueled genocide and the most violent struggles imaginable. In 2016, Guyana will celebrate fifty years of independence. Though there are many disappointments in this half century, a stable transition between ruling parties (in May 2015) augurs well as an auspicious sign for this anniversary, and might even signal the future the President and ruling coalition envisions of Guyana becoming once again a magnet for its own diaspora.

Many of Guyana's citizens, writers, politicians and intellectuals have been wise enough to see beyond ethnic divisions. The government in power has prudently displayed a willingness to work with their major opposition the PPP and display a propensity to collaborate in some areas with shared governance without compromising the stated electoral will of the Guyanese people; thus helping to make the PPP more comfortable with its opposition status.

The virtue of this decision is that the Guyanese electorate has made a definitive choice for their leaders peacefully, and this accord would allow all leaders to honor the results of the last election, giving the society the chance to become increasingly more inclusive and unified across ethic divisions.

The intersection of major conflicting challenges

When the economic malaise the Guyanese nation has suffered is unpacked, its burden of foreign debt looms large as an impediment. It is clear that this burden impedes actions such as the import of spare parts, raw materials and equipment. Seriously hampered as well is the replacement of decaying industrial stock, agricultural, manufacturing equipment and a host of other critical resources this relatively young developing country needs for its sustenance, continuous viability and development.

Few can doubt that the Guyanese diaspora can have an important dynamic role by assisting in alleviating these challenges and helping to spur national and regional development. Fortunately, Guyana's new leaders have acknowledged the presence of the diaspora and must now continue to court and utilize this tremendously important, potentially resource-rich population in national development.

It is well recognized that the growing diaspora is a consequence of a mass exodus of students, intellectuals, and qualified experts, representing a talent drain from various occupational fields. During the political upheavals experienced in the nation, many citizens migrated overseas during one crisis or another for economic reasons, to further their education or in search of better health outcomes for persistent illnesses. The resulting outcome has been a serious depletion of human talent. This continues to weaken institutional and national talent pools.

Driven by a strong desire for self-empowerment, many migrating Guyanese have become substantially skilled professionals who have enhanced their capabilities and expertise through further educational and working experiences found more readily abroad. Having achieved self-actualization (wholly or in part) they have become a willing cadre of talented nationals willing to give back to their ancestral homeland.

Guyana's leaders will be prudent to continue to engage individuals and organizations in the diaspora to encourage a repatriation process to attract as many diaspora residents as able to support continuing national rebuilding and developmental processes. This can be accomplished through a number of local, regional and international efforts to bring back the diaspora to support the nation-building process.

These efforts can be fueled by efforts to capitalize on social and patriotic linkages to establish and deepen relationships that encourage the diaspora to invest in national development and national institutional capacity building. Many of these relationships already exist among diaspora residents who have long been involved in Guyana's national economic growth through their remittances, exports of scarce products and medical supplies.

Dispersed, hit or miss efforts, need to be organized into a focused intensive development thrust. Such a major program must be supported with financial and other critical resources to become successful. Guyana can learn important lessons from other countries such as China, Korea, India and countries in Africa, that have utilized the contributions of diaspora residents in national development.

These countries have been exceptionally successful in demonstrating that diaspora contributions can significantly help to transform economies. Their strategies illustrate the success of nationally engineered initiatives that are instigated using paradigms of shared development objectives between the government and the diaspora. Key tactics include the work of collaborative participating groups, comprehensive policies, administrative structures and motivating incentives to foster enabling conditions for leveraging diaspora resources (expertise, investments, entrepreneurship and corporate affiliations) around critical growth pillars.

This publication proposes and promotes the important model titled "A FUN Blueprint for diaspora engagement in national development." The model utilizes the diaspora in building international and domestic institutional capacity for strengthening management of national development, reconstruction and sustainable development projects on the whole. The FUN Blueprint is based on the collaboration and participation of both national representatives as well as diaspora professionals in multiple fields. Each will utilize general and specific professional knowledge in areas of critically needed expertise.

The Need for Development Capital

The strategies of diaspora collaboration and participation work best when diaspora constituents are not merely considered sources of financing, but as developmental partners. The urgency of building stronger relationships between nationally based partners and diaspora based constituents groups cannot be overstated. Local banks, overseas banks and other funding sources need to be involved as critical partners.

Several international agencies stand ready to assist in this effort; they include the United Nations Development Program (UNDP), USAID, the World Health Organization (WHO), United Nations International Children's Emergency Fund (UNICEF), the Food and Agriculture Organization (FAO), and the World Food Program. Multilateral agencies that deal primarily in financial resource transfer need to be included in this effort. Some with a history of funding such programs include the World Bank

(International Development Agency and International Bank for Reconstruction and Development), and the Foundation for Agricultural Development.

Other groups are the Consultative Group on International Agricultural Research consortium and others dealing with specialized developmental issues and problems; among these is the Swedish Agency for Research Cooperation with Developing Countries, the International Development Research Centre of Canada, and the Australian Development Assistance Bureau. The assistance of these public agencies may be complimented by the private efforts of foundations, international voluntary agencies, and other institutions. Major private American foundations engaged in development work include foundations like Ford, Rockefeller, and Carnegie; and several new foundations emerging in the United States, Europe, and Japan. Some of the most visible are international voluntary agencies such as CARE, Catholic

Relief Services, and Oxfam. These public and private agencies are often enjoined with research universities conducting research in disciplinary fields including nutrition-related fields of public health, agriculture, economics, and management.

Guyana has in the past, and even currently, sought limited programs with a few of these agencies. However, the current diaspora development initiative calls for a broader, more comprehensive and deeper engagement with these principals, focused on a concentrated thrust on national development and sustainability. Following the guidance of the 'FUN Blueprint' a Diaspora Engagement Network, (henceforth referred to as the DEN), is a useful place to start.

The DEN brings together fundraisers and grant writers, and diaspora volunteers. This group will be mobilized and empowered with the help of grant and fund raising specialists to develop grant applications and associated vehicles to garner substantial funding and partnership with agencies that have a track record in this work.

Financial partners can provide technical assistance and financial support for developmental initiatives, and work with diaspora and national partners to create enabling environments for mainstreaming diaspora contributions for significant economic transitions. Diaspora and national governmental collaboration is more effective when established as comprehensive national strategies, instead of ad hoc projects. Consistent with the proposed FUN Blueprint model, the financing needed for the collaborative venture needs to be leveraged, such that the financiers could use their investments to spur diaspora financial contributions for entrepreneurship and private sector growth in the nation.

Additionally, a task force on diaspora and remittances could explore together, with the Treasury Departments of partnership banks, the issuance of diaspora development bonds. The funding raised through grants from these multiple agencies will comprise the Guyana Diaspora Fund identified in the FUN Blueprint. Additional sources of funding will be contributed from periodic funding efforts of the DEN.

The manpower needs could be satisfied as highly qualified experts in the diaspora are engaged without the need for physical relocation or as dual citizens. The Guyana Government needs to consider granting dual citizenship to all diaspora residents who desire it as motivation for their contribution to national development. In this way, diaspora members can be nurtured as network participants instead of as separate individuals, and enabled to render services through direct contact as well as through virtual interaction and social media among other communication resources.

This model of collaborative national development with national leaders and constituent diaspora groups will capitalize on networks of kinship and language. These elements facilitate interaction across national boundaries by speeding the flow of information between partners.

Kinship relationships foster trust and a knowledge of how the local culture supports collaborative processes and interaction. Diaspora residents can assist in bridging many cultural divides. Guyanese in the diaspora have who have been educated in the Caribbean and abroad have acquired exceptional skills that can be useful to the effort. Some of them have eventually returned to their homeland taking with them both knowledge and contacts that can help fuel the type of collaborative relationships discussed here.

There is little doubt that entrepreneurs in the diaspora can contribute significantly and effectively to economic development in Guyana. Through direct investment in Guyana,. diaspora entrepreneurs can play an important role in initiating development projects in a variety of areas. Such projects can foster business development, job creation, competition, innovation, and the creation of transnational business networks. These can also merge with existing social capital in diaspora communities and in turn generate new opportunities for sharing economic, social, and political capital. These opportunities can spread through global networks for creating entrepreneurial activities with the greatest potential for creating new and novel online technological economic activities.

Diaspora involvement in economic development can advance computer and related entrepreneurship. The latter can increase the vibrancy of economic activity and lead to higher levels of networked technological online entrepreneurship. Technological entrepreneurship activities can stimulate economic growth and national economic development on a wide scale. The proposed FUN Blueprint for diaspora engagement in national development serves as a framework and networking system that organizes and integrate these elements together as a focused developmental tool.

5 FOUNDATIONAL PREMISES

One of the most critical features of the FUN Blueprint is the emotive component. This component is an affective component of joyful, caring and prideful involvement. Reference to the Blueprint illustration above shows that this is the largest component and is represented within the circle as shown. For the most part, the Guyanese diaspora is committed to stimulating positive economic, sociocultural, and political aspirations, resulting in a sense of security, a feeling of belonging, and pride in their accomplishment and contributions.

While these emotive needs are regarded as universal, their strength can be motivational in influencing diaspora groups to be dedicated to constructive involvement in national development. The underlying needs for attachment must necessarily embrace all ethnic groups identifying as Guyanese; thus assisting in overcoming ethnic cleavages.

Personal relevance becomes an important value for individuals involved in national development work. Attachment to the homeland reinforces their motivation to come together and collectively help their country. This activity in turn further deepens their sense of identity and self-esteem through their shared, mutual, national identification and engagement.

The Guyana Diaspora's contribution as agents of Guyana's socio-economic change should not be measured merely as inputs of skilled labor. Their contribution to development also lies in the ability of the diaspora to build bridges between Guyana and the diaspora that help to stimulate, not only economic activity, but transfers of knowledge, cultural and social norms. Given this context

Diaspora Engagement serves to:

• Facilitate a Needs Assessment/Survey of the Guyana diaspora focused on their views, aspirations, their skills, occupations and their potential for participation in national development. Detailed information on the diaspora that would enable the formulation of informed policies and related action

• Facilitate the establishment of a database of key stakeholders to help facilitate the transfer of knowledge and skills to Guyana

• Create greater awareness of Guyana's development issues

• Actively stimulate engagement in Guyana's development

• Forge stronger connections with local development initiatives in Guyana and the diaspora

• Increase its collaboration with Guyana diaspora groups in the US, Canada, the United Kingdom, Europe and the Caribbean to collaborate in

development and other national building efforts
in collaboration with overseas interests

- Contribute to the increasingly irrefutable evidence and recognition of the potential value that the Guyana Diaspora brings to development efforts in the nation of Guyana

- Engender collaborative capacity building in form of partnerships, networks and exchanges of skills and knowledge between the Guyanese diaspora and local development initiatives in Guyana to create sustainable development.

Diaspora Needs Assessment/Survey

A first step in implementing this Blueprint is a Guyana Diaspora Needs/Assessment Survey. An example of the kind of survey envisaged can be found in Appendix B. (It is an example of an empirical tool created for mobilizing the Guyanese Diaspora.) A survey and needs assessment of this kind can provide the data, information, skills and knowledge of the diaspora that forms some of the major critical resources and ingredients that are essential for the appropriate implementation of the recommended Blueprint.

This FUN Blueprint and needs assessment survey are tools or strategic planning devices for organizing for effective results. The Blueprint structures a process of group participation in planning, engagement, goal setting, objective accomplishment, assessment and evaluation that considers the group's purpose, capacities and environment, and results in a series of strategic action phases. Blueprint action plans inevitably determine a path for development of the group's resources in order to achieve meaningful results.

This type of participative planning and implementation represents engagement for significant change. It is dynamic and proactive. It stimulates change, rather than simply reacts to it. It also builds in accountability by incorporating ways to assess progress toward targeted outcomes. It is adaptable and allows, assessment, revision and improvement.

The flexibility of the Blueprint accommodates long-range approaches but utilizes regular reviews and updates to analyze progress and needed adjustments in response to changing circumstances and emerging opportunities. The FUN Blueprint for strategic diaspora engagement employs common sense. It is visionary yet realistic; it illustrates a future that is both desirable and achievable. It provides a structure for inspired but practical decision-making and follow-through. The FUN Blueprint is a guide for good management. It involves a disciplined effort to help shape and guide what the diaspora does and why it does it. It requires broad-scale information gathering, exploration of alternatives, and emphasis on the future implications of current decisions. It facilitates communication and participation, accommodates divergent interests and values, and fosters orderly, informed decision-making and successful implementation.

Applying the Blueprint for national development

To facilitate an effective plan for engagement and national development the diaspora must have a heightened awareness of national development goals. With this insight they can accept their roles as a collaborating group that can help to assist and promote those that are viable, or suggest alternate goals that reflect high feasibility. The FUN Blueprint helps to examine what opportunities for change exist. (For example, what are the national priorities for change that Guyana's leaders envisage, and what roles can diaspora volunteers play in advancing these?) It also raises associated questions such as,

How does the diaspora participant group identify with these priorities?

Answers to these important interrogatories help to determine the extent of diaspora support and involvement. Successful blueprint implementation efforts involve tactical and deliberate planning, application, monitoring, and evaluation (these steps will ultimately provide data that will be used in future planning and implementation efforts). Strategic Blueprint implementation planning is an essential first step in the development of a results-based accountability system. This system can be defined as the process of addressing the following questions:

- Where are we with respect to diaspora engagement?

- What resources do we have to work with for successful diaspora engagement?

- Where do we want to be in our diaspora engagement efforts?

- How do we become fully engaged in diaspora engagement?

- How do we assess our progress and results from diaspora engagement?

This process is undertaken step by step, and by assessing each step for quality and effectiveness.

The steps involved in implementing this strategic FUN Blueprint are described below. Although this process is systematic and rational, it is also iterative and evolves substantially over time. Further, it is subject to external influences and needs to be modified accordingly. Implementation efforts may include minor adjustments to the steps described.

Blueprint Planning and engagement Processes

The first step in the strategic FUN Blueprint planning process is to address questions such as:

A. "Who are we (What is our connection to Guyana?)"

B. "What is our occupation/profession?"

C. "What skill levels do we have for our engagement in homeland (Guyana) development activities (HDA)?"

D. "Why do we want to be engaged in homeland developmental activities?"

E. "What is our project for diaspora engagement?"

F. "How is this aligned to national developmental goals?"

G. "What resources are needed for this project?

Next, participants may take into account the recent history and changing contexts (both internal and external) of the diaspora collaborative group, program, or sub-program. This allows an assessment of the current environment for diaspora engagement. Answering the question of what do we have to work with, with respect to diaspora engagement, involves consideration of resources, strengths and weaknesses and a determination of how to capitalize on strengths, while overcoming or reducing weaknesses.

The first step in the process, helps to identify the origins of team members with respect to their citizenship status or other relationship to Guyana and the country's national interests.

As the articulated vision stems from the values of those involved in the process, it is essential that this step involve all of those who will have a stake in achieving the vision. For collaborative groups, the vision is then translated into a mission statement: a broad, comprehensive statement of the purpose of the group or program. It is useful for the group to design mission statements that can encompass multiple divergent goals. Group leaders may lead group members to articulate several separate mission statements reflecting different combination of goals prior to choosing one that gets the consensus approval.

The next step in the planning process is the articulation of goals. Desired long-range conditions of achievement for the collaborative initiative. Such goals indicate the intended future direction of the initiative, or program.

After articulating the vision and determining goals, following the blueprint steps, the participating group must address all means of reaching their goals. This step involves articulating strategies for achieving results. Strategies should reflect the strengths and weaknesses of the entity engaged in the planning. Recognition of relative strengths and weaknesses is helpful in identifying promising strategies.

The blueprint includes consideration of methods of goal measurement. Addressing goal measurement involves articulation of objectives, indicators, and benchmarks. Objectives are the short-term conditions needed to achieve desired conditions of achievement for the initiative in the long term. Indicators are quantifiable measures of progress; they should provide numeric assessment of the desired conditions of goal attainment. Benchmarks are target levels of performance expressed in measurable terms and specified time frames.

Useful Steps may focus on conducting:

• A Diaspora Needs Assessment Survey to build a Diaspora Professionals' Skills Database

• Developing a National/Diaspora outreach campaign (Provide dual-citizenship for Guyanese in the diaspora through negotiation)

• Hosting conferences and visits (in Guyana and in diaspora communities)

• Developing and enhancing dialogue with the diaspora

• Hosting a discussion of national interests, development priorities (and roles for the diaspora)

• Engaging in trust building exercises

• Promoting conditions to maximize diaspora potential

• Promoting respect for diaspora rights (reduce vulnerability, including, Property rights – Social protection & access to essential services)

• Facilitating trade & Investment

• Strengthening institutional frameworks – Integrate diaspora policies into national development plans

• Engaging in institution building

• Conducting training of project participants (include both diaspora volunteers and national participants)

• Conducting overseas voter registration and allowing qualified diaspora voters to vote

• Establishing a Guyanese Diaspora Volunteers Corps

• Establishing a Guyanese Diaspora Investment Fund

• Establishing a Diaspora Development Marketplace for facilitating innovation and entrepreneurship between Guyana and Diaspora

• Establishing a Guyanese Remittances Institute

• Institutionalizing the permanent and temporary skills transfer of highly qualified Guyanese

• Establishing a website devoted exclusively to diaspora engagement concerns, national development updates and related matters.

6 USING THE FUN BLUEPRINT WITH GROUPS

To initiate the use of the blueprint to engage groups in the planning and engagement process, one approach is to follow and implement the guidance provided here.

Step One: The group designates the FUN Blueprint for Strategic Planning, (BSP) with a Coordinator in the lead role.

Step Two: Initiate an internal/external assessment under the coordination of the BSP Coordinator with input from various levels of the Diaspora Collaborative Group (DCG) and external stakeholders.

Step Three: Articulate a shared vision for the DCG after several rounds of meetings with group members and national stakeholders. The BSP and DCG define the group's mission and express the group's philosophy (reflecting the group's vision of service excellence or core values).

Step Four: Establish and rank DCG goals, based on careful consideration of external factors and internal capacities (revealed in the internal/external assessment) with the BSP Coordinator and DCG.

Step Five: Communicate the DCG mission, philosophy, and goals to every level of the DCG sub groups.

Step Six: Define DCG program missions, express program philosophies, and establish program goals (based on internal/external assessment, including input from front-line employees and consideration of resources needed for achievement) that are consistent.

Step Seven: Work with DCG members, program managers and key staff members (including or with input from budget managers and key fiscal staff, facility managers, human resource managers, information systems managers, and front-line supervisors) to develop measurable objectives for each activity, build strategies, and identify resources necessary to implement strategies and accomplish objectives. However, objectives and strategies should be considered "tentative" or "proposed" until input is received from the front-line personnel who will bear the responsibility for carrying out strategies and operationalizing them through action plans.

Step Eight: Feedback and rollup begin. Within each program, work with lower levels to submit plan elements to the next higher management level for review and coordination. After revisions (if any) are made, incorporate planned actions into the appropriate portion of the program strategic plan. During feedback and rollup, it may be necessary to revise objectives or strategies originally proposed. For example, input from front-line levels may show that the time frame or resource allocation originally projected for a particular strategy should be changed. As strategies are detailed and delineated it may become apparent that the time frame or degree of change proposed in an objective should be altered.

Step Nine: Working with program managers combine all elements into a program strategic plan and submit this plan, through the planning coordinator, to the BSP, DCG and national representatives for review and coordination.

Step Ten: Review program plans with the BSP Coordinator and DCG. They identify opportunities for coordination among programs plans and any conflicts among program plans are worked out. This review may drive development of DCG-wide objectives. When the DSC and BSP Coordinator determine that a program plan must be revised, clear feedback to the program manager and staff is provided. The BSP Coordinator and DCG pinpoint the efforts they must make to support program plans and help to overcome hurdles to accomplishing objectives.

Step Eleven: The BSP Coordinator assists in coordinating program plans into a DCG Blueprint strategic plan.

Step Twelve: The DCG puts the blueprint strategic plan into action. The plan guides both operational planning, and capital outlay planning and budgeting. Strategic and operational progress is regularly evaluated and the plan is revised accordingly. Successes are celebrated and rewarded; lack of progress is analyzed, lessons are learned, and appropriate changes made.

Initiating a typical development initiative

Each diaspora development initiative or program should, at a minimum, comprise:

A Name (e.g. *Diaspora Action & Marketplace for Effective Development DAME*)

1. A strategic plan (Vision, Mission, Goals, Objectives and activities)

2. A brief statement identifying the principal clients and users of each program of the initiative, and the specific service or benefit derived by such persons

3. An identification of potential external factors that are beyond the control of the Diaspora Collaborative Group (DCG) that could significantly affect the achievement of its goals and objectives.

4. A statement of each strategy that the DCG will use in achieving each stated goal and objective

5. An explanation of how duplication of effort will be avoided When the operations of more than one program are directed at achieving a single goal, objective, or strategy

6.   Specific and measurable performance indicators for each objective

7.   A description of specific program assessments and evaluations used to develop objectives and strategies

8.   Program descriptive information, including organization charts, and program Zeitgeiste

Program Evaluation:

The FUN Blueprint for Strategic Diaspora Engagement (BSDE) plans must be carried down to the program level; program evaluation, revisions and updates are integral components. Distribution of revised (BSDE) plans should follow the same guidelines as cited earlier for initial strategic plans. (BSDE) plans review compares actual with expected results; it looks at projected versus actual timetables.

It determines whether the plan is on time and on target.

Annual progress evaluation allows all program participants (from the diaspora as well as those representing national interests) to what is changing internally and externally, as well as, what parts of the plan are progressing smoothly or those that are not progressing as expected. The collaborative group is then armed with empirical data to update (BSDE) plans.

An effective review can reveal how well the program is reaching its intended goals. These contingencies may reveal that:

- There are no major changes in internal capacity or external operating environment;
- Strategies and action plans are proceeding on schedule;
- Progress toward goals and objectives is being realized as expected; and anticipated results are being achieved;

Following the review and evaluation, the collaborative group reaffirms goals, objectives, and strategies. If necessary appropriate adjustments may become necessary to each of these stages as the plan moves ahead. If the review and evaluation stages may show that there are significant changes in the internal capacity or external operating environment. This may result in changes in strategies and in action plans.

Revising and Updating the Plan

To review, revise, and update a strategic plan, it is important to take a look at each of the plan components and determine whether each is still valid. Relevant questions to guide this process may approximate the following:

- Has there been any significant changes in the collaborative group internal capacity? For example:

- Has the collaborative group's mission changed? Have the goals changed?

- Has the collaborative group's program been assigned or undertaken any new responsibilities? If so, what are they and how will they affect mission and goals?

- Has the budget or position allocations changed significantly?

- Has the organization undergone reorganization?

- Has administrative procedures or guidelines been revised significantly?

- Has the organization received significant or repeated audit findings?

- Were there major changes in the organization's external operating environment?

For example:

- Were new mandates placed on the collaborative group?

- Have new public issues surfaced that are related to the collaborative group?

- Has there been economic, demographic, political, environmental, or societal shifts that will affect the organization and its mission?

- Has national policy and the national collaborative group established goals, objectives, or strategies that must be incorporated into the program's BSDE plan?

- Has the collaborative group's enabling mission or other goals been changed? If so, what changed and how will those changes affect objectives and activities?

- Has the collaborative group's program been assigned or undertaken any new responsibilities? If so, what are they and how will they affect mission and goals?

- Are objectives, strategies, and action plans on schedule and fulfilling expectations?

- If so, how can the collaborative group build on this progress?

- If more progress than expected has been made, should objectives be set higher?

- If less progress than expected has been made, should objectives be lowered or extended in time?

- Should strategies be revised, overhauled, or thrown out entirely?

- Are other changes required to allow the organization to make progress?

- Are performance indicators capturing the information necessary to chart progress and support management decision-making?

- Does each activity include at least one outcome-based performance indicator? If not, what changes are needed?

Incentives for Guyanese nationals in the diaspora

The participation of diaspora residents is hardly solely altruistic. There are benefits that the government could offer to all investors. Fiscal incentives include exemptions from customs duties on construction machinery, equipment and building materials required for investment, depending on the types of investment, as well as production machinery and equipment. Income tax exemption should also be available for developers and resident firms based on international best practices.

The Guyanese diaspora can benefit from investing in their country thereby sustaining ongoing development endeavors. Such development ventures can create a variety of jobs for youth and women, thus helping to lift millions from poverty. The latter can have the longer-term benefit of changing the mindset of youth and young adults who may aspire to flee the country because of lack of opportunities for their personal development. This can perpetuate the continuing cycle of talent drain and underdevelopment that has been evidenced for many years. Two actions that can strengthen diaspora engagement are building a community of interests and exploring the possibility of diaspora residents obtaining dual citizenship.

Dual citizenship of Guyana diaspora members residing in the US can allow them to have two passports and access to the social service systems. These dual citizens have access to the same set of opportunities in two countries. For example, citizens may be allowed to vote in both countries.

They can be allowed to work in both countries. Working in the country with better wages or conditions helps to facilitate their engagement in development initiatives in Guyana. The advantage of owning property in both countries can likewise help the Guyanese diaspora members overcome the barriers of finding reliable lodgings for periodic stays in Guyana when they visit to engage in development work.

Pride, loyalty and a sense of belonging

Diaspora members who are dual citizens can legally carry two passports and feel confident that they belong and are welcome in both countries. They can embrace Guyana as their homeland and the US as a new home, and fully embrace and experience the ideals of both, while strengthening both cultural and political loyalty to both; thus feeling welcome in both societies.

Promoting cultural education

Their dual citizenship would provide Guyanese diaspora members with the chance to educate others about the culture and societies of two different nations. Dual citizenship status would also assist diaspora members to promote Guyana's image and culture abroad. With two passports, diaspora members may have more access to the world and be encouraged with broadened perspectives of how best to engage effectively in national development.

Having ease of travel when travelling abroad for development work or vacation, diaspora members, who are dual citizens, can enjoy the protection of two governments. Whether traveling for development work or vacation, they can appeal to one or both governments' embassies in case of issues or problems during such trips.

Diaspora Contributions to national development

These contributions may occur in the following areas,

- Leveraging human & social capital

- Transferring skills and knowledge

- Building extended development economic and capital networks

- Creating dynamic enterprises rather than merely sending remittances and savings

- Creating cultural, and capital trade and investment programs

- Engineering societies that are dynamic and innovative

- Enhancing reliable and sustainable relations between countries

Benefits of implementing the Blueprint include,

- Initiating Investment clubs of diaspora residents and

- Growing and expanding educational opportunities on the condition that award holders contribute to national development projects.

7 BENEFICIAL PROJECTS

Selecting beneficial projects

Various forms of energy are among the essential resources for economic development whether in developing countries or more developed countries. Certainly in less developed countries, such as Guyana, the extent of development and continuing development is directly linked to access of affordable sources of energy. Developing countries like Guyana are in the desperate position of depending on costly and harmful fossil fuels, like oil, as fuel for economic development. In these countries, often the most rural regions are agricultural and depend partly on firewood for cooking and agricultural power as well on human and animal muscle for mechanical power. Other viable industries in Guyana are the mining industries. Among the mineral rich Guyana deposits, are substantial mineral deposits that have attracted international interest from the largest mining companies in the world. Those such as bauxite, gold, and diamonds have been traditionally and currently exploited with accompanying damage to the local environment and infrastructure.

The mineral riches of Guyana also include deposits of semi-precious stones, such as laterite, manganese, kaolin, sand resources, radioactive minerals, copper, molybdenum, tungsten, iron, and nickel as well as others that are lesser known. Mining in Guyana is an important economic industry that contributes significantly to the economy of Guyana, but suffers from the same lack of modernization, development, and unfair practices as with other important economic sectors. Guyana, like other developing countries, has the potential for the development of abundant renewable energy resources for its own use and for export. Mineral and energy surveys over the years have confirmed the possibility of vast, largely unexploited, resources such as hydro electricity, solar energy, wind power, geothermal energy, natural-gas and biomass reserves.

The nation also possesses relatively labor-intensive systems to harness these and make them viable. By developing these tremendous energy reserves Guyana can reduce or sever its dependence on oil and other fossil fuels, while creating energy portfolios that are far less vulnerable to price fluctuations and increases.

These investments are certainly less expensive and harmful to the environment than fossil fuel energy systems. In time, they have then potential to make the nation a primary producer of energy for its own development. Added to this possibility, the nation can become a major exporter of energy to the other proximate Caribbean, Latin American and other regions internationally that suffer a shortage of energy. With a robust renewable energy industry, Guyana will definitely contribute to the alleviation of poverty by providing the energy needed for stimulating and creating businesses, for expanding employment and for sustainability.

The educational sector can benefit by assuming the responsibility for the provision of needed technical skills and

advanced training in areas hitherto excluded or missing from the curricula of most national academies. By far the greatest benefit is the reduction of exorbitant costs of resources for lighting, manufacturing, other industrial and collateral needs.

The health of the nation can improve overall when energy is provided for the refrigeration of medicine and the sterilization or medical equipment in rural areas where the access to electricity is sporadic or difficult. It can also provide energy to supply fresh water and needed sewerage facilities to reduce the spread of infectious diseases.

Government Renewable Energy Policies

By the development of robust renewable energy technologies, for internal and external and markets, Guyana can compete well with other energy exporting countries in the Caribbean, Latin America, and North America that have traditionally provided the energy needs in the hemisphere. Meticulously crafted policies will be needed to steer resources, mobilize large-scale investments and steer the transition into new productive sectors and technologies.

Strategic actions would be needed to craft industrial policies that can combine large-scale investments and commensurate policy interventions. Such energy products and services need to be set to affordable prices accessible to the populations in various regions of the nation.

8 OBSTACLES TO DIASPORA ENGAGEMENT

The Affective Component

The motivation to engage in national development as a member of the diaspora is partly associated with affective feelings. This includes positive emotive feelings such as kinship, national pride, national identity, patriotism, and other personal positive expressions that demonstrate support for the national Zeitgeiste, or well-being. The absence of these positive feelings for the nation may affect the extent to which Guyanese in the diaspora are willing to become involved in their country's national development.

An appropriate strategy to begin the engagement of the

diaspora in national development work would be to stimulate those feelings of national identity, pride and national affinity for the homeland. It is this context of national pride and affinity that will provide answers to the question of "Why should I become engaged?"

This strategy underscores the effectiveness presence of the affective component of diaspora engagement. This component provides a rationale for diaspora engagement while answering another question. That is the question of "Why should I care?" When the answer to this question is "Because of my national affinity, as a citizen of Guyana, and my love for my homeland," a compelling narrative is created that justifies any amount of time and resources devoted to the cause. In short, it becomes important to the diaspora to be so engaged because of these intrinsic feelings and motivations. An important sub-model of diaspora engagement is displayed below, based on the concepts of:

- Why?
- How? and
- What?
- Why?

The question of: Why should the diaspora become engaged in

national development is answered by the following logical and

strategic rationale.

A commitment to engagement is the next logical step after a

commitment and demonstration of pride, patriotism and confidence

that the potential viability of the nation can be realized by the

collective efforts of Guyanese whether they reside in Guyana or in

the diaspora. Driven by their national affinity, pride and patriotism all

Guyanese, can exercise their debt to the nation by their commitment

and in national development.

How?

The FUN Blueprint for diaspora engagement as illustrated above

shows how the diaspora may implement a comprehensive sequential

approach to diaspora engagement.

After completing the first step by completing a needsassessment and

comprehensive survey of diaspora capabilities, skills, professions, and

willingness to engage in the meticulous work of national

development, the group is armed with important resources to

proceed to the next sequential steps.

As stated earlier, the data and information collected will help to create an affective context for national development and provide the motivation for engagement.

What?

By evoking kinship - the belief or the feeling of belonging or attachment to the nation, nationalism or national identity becomes a driving force for engagement. As the work on development continues diaspora members will naturally gain a sense of pride in their part for improving conditions in their beloved nation. In this manner, initial successes can build on other sequential successes as the work continues; however, as the work of development is undertaken it is important to become aware of the obstacles to engagement.

Obstacles to Engagement

While the affective component of the Blueprint is a powerful motivational and unifying rationale for engagement in diaspora engagement, other serious obstacles that cannot be ignored exist.

Indeed some commentators have voiced viewpoint that though desirable, diaspora engagement in national development is just not an important priority to leaders in the government or persons in the diaspora. These voices fear that though often articulated, diaspora engagement is much too frequently considered a side issue rather than a central issue of governance. For this reason, they doubt that serious time and resources will be readily devoted to this cause. They argue that the rewards from engagement efforts are tenuous at best and outcomes are slow to be realized for the most part. Further, that when stacked up against the plethora of urgent needs of a developing country, leaders will naturally prefer to solve the urgent and immediate contentious issues that threaten their powerbase rather than flirt with the diaspora and the uncertainties of national development initiatives.

Another argument is that though diaspora engagement in national development is too often expressed theoretically, in practice it is difficult to rally diaspora members of divergent interests, capabilities and commitment around the cause of development.

In the face of greater, more urgent priorities, it is often said that "people will just talk about it, then do nothing." This attitude can be overcome by reminding diaspora and national audiences of the "why" (explained above) and of the "benefits" of development. Another method for guaranteeing diaspora engagement is the strategy of involving diaspora members early in the process of planning development efforts and identifying roles clearly. This eventually leads to their recruitment as willing and essential engaged partners.

Some of the hallmarks and benefits of development include structural change, sustainability, and the reduction of dependence on more developed countries. Added to this are changing economic models from those of a developing economy primarily composed of agricultural and mining industries to a more robust, modern, more urbanized, and a more industrially diverse manufacturing and service economy is seen.

It also includes a diverse economy where international trade, fair court systems, available medical care, education, equality, high employment and political freedom flourishes.

Complementing these values are the manufacture and adoption of the latest technology and entrepreneurship, higher productivity levels and one where modern economic growth is displayed.

All national development requires some basic funding. To implement development initiatives at sufficient levels, funding is essential. While multiple sectors and cross-jurisdictional partnerships are often key to successful community and economic development, there are many real obstacles to diaspora engagement. Those who have been, for some time, engaged in sending scarce products to Guyana have an inclination to protect their own turf, time, and trust. Others may naturally resist changes to the status quo, tend to want to protect their own turf, and are reluctant to share power and control.

An urgent need is to improve the chances of diaspora and collaborative success through increasing partnership opportunities. A key skill involved in this, is the diaspora leader's ability to cultivate and manage relationships. At the heart of this competency is a cluster of personal attributes. One of these is what psychologists now call "emotional intelligence." A lack of emotional intelligence often manifests as a lack of trust between potential partners. This could be due to experiences in the past that lead to mistrust, or it could be a lack of knowledge of each other on the part of collaborating partners. In either case, the root problem is usually relational. The concern here may be the extent to which potential partners know and trust one another.

The development effort may well depend on the success of the diaspora at building and maintaining relationships of trust between diaspora members and national groups. Though engagement leaders may have the requisite level of technical capabilities, those qualities alone are not sufficient for leadership. Diaspora and national partners need to have a sufficient level of emotional intelligence to make their partnership successful. In this respect, the emotional intelligence required comprises five components according to Daniel Coleman.[2]

> **"Self-Awareness,** which involves understanding how others see you, having self confidence, and realistic self-assessment;
>
> **Regulation,** which involves being able to control disruptive impulses, being open to change,

---

[2] Coleman, Daniel. *Emotional Intelligence.* New York: Bantam Books, 1995.

comfortable with ambiguity, able to suspend judgment, and ultimately, personal integrity;

Motivation, which involves a passion for outcomes beyond status or wealth, optimism, and commitment;

Empathy, which is the ability to understand others' emotions and being sensitive to that (some would also include a service ethic here); and

Social Skills, which include networking, building relationships, working with others, and being able to find common ground among different interests."

According to Coleman these components of emotional intelligence (EQ) are strongly linked to effective leadership in a general manner. More importantly however, they are particularly relevant to leadership for diaspora engagement and overcoming the relational obstacles inherent in most of the needed partnerships.

To implement the highest levels of collaborative engagement, it is important to ensure the highest levels of emotional intelligence among partners. It is an essential skill that can be learned or developed, (if not already present). Though it increases with age and experience, it can also be purposely developed. Deliberate attempts to foster emotional intelligence would include activities that promote sharing, feedback, and coaching. Obstacles to collaborative diaspora engagement can be overcome with high "EQs," and strong team leadership.

9 EXAMPLES OF DIASPORA ENGAGEMENT

Examples of Diaspora Engagement

Leaders and policymakers in the Asia-Pacific region increasingly recognize the value that diaspora populations bring to development efforts in nation states. Some governments in the region have taken an extra step in reinforcing their engagement with the diaspora by creating agencies or executive boards within governmental agencies. By the end of the nineteenth century, fourteen governmental agencies in Asia were created specifically to involve diasporas formally. These were established with various levels of government and demonstrated multiple priorities and types of institutions devoted to working on development projects with nation states.

Other countries such as India, have placed the needs of diaspora populations within ministries. In the case of India, the major agency for diaspora engagement is the Overseas Ministry for Overseas Indian Affairs. Formed in 2004, the responsibility of this ministry is to formulate government policies, coordinate migration, and to establish programs and policies to engage the Indian diaspora. Bangladesh and Sri Lanka also have followed India by also founding ministries to engage and work in partnership with their diasporas.

In some Asian countries, diaspora agencies have not attained the status of ministries. They are however, still the responsibility of the highest government executive body. In this manner, they occupy a position of importance within the government. A case in point is the Overseas Chinese Affairs Office. In addition to working with the diaspora, this office manages two universities devoted to the Chinese diaspora. Like the above Indian examples, this office reports to the state council. The latter is the highest executive body of the country.

Like the above examples, the Philippines Commission on has reporting responsibilities to the Office of the President Filipinos. The Commission was established in 1980. Its dual role is to promote both economic and cultural ties between the Philippines and its diaspora. Additionally, the government has created three special offices reporting to the departments of labor and employment and foreign affairs.

For many of these countries engagement with the diaspora is not restricted at the national level. They utilize kinship and family ties to be involved at the local level where close relationships with the diaspora are present. In contrast, the South Korean foundation, founded in 1977 for diaspora engagement is indirectly outside the ambit of government. This nonprofit foundation is only loosely associated with the ministry of foreign affairs and trade. Its clear mission is to utilize the talents and capabilities of the Korean diaspora for national development and to promote its globalization interests and policies.

While many governments acknowledge the importance of diaspora engagement in development, many still lack the capacity to design effective policies and implement them on a meaningful scale. This explains the gap between schemes that look good on

paper and truly effective policies and programs that actually make a difference. Indeed, effective engagement almost always requires a conrcerted effort towards capacity building.

Internationally, many countries in Asia and elsewhere have major challenges so far as diaspora engagement is concerned. Among the many challenges, two are of particular concern.

1)   Obtaining the funding necessary to sustain robust and effective diaspora engagement

2)   Obtaining the technical knowledge of fully organizing and productively engaging the diaspora

To be maximally effective, a successful model for diaspora engagement must consist of logical steps, that utilize pertinent data and information from the diaspora. and of the global are critical for the country's development. Continuous monitoring, review, evaluation and adjustment via a feedback loop are essential as illustrated in the Blueprint.

10 DIASPORA ENGAGEMENT FUNDING

Diaspora Engagement Funding

Main sources of income for the Diaspora Engagement Network (DEN) would include donations and gifts, fundraisers (such as a bi-annual gala, fund raising dinners and other periodic fundraisers). Additionally the sale of diaspora treasury bonds, grants and other collateral fund raising strategies will be pursued.

Donations and Gifts

Donations and gifts are a particularly valuable source of income for the proposed diaspora engagement fund and can benefit the donors through the tax relief they can earn. Donations and gifts can benefit the DEN by funding it to provide help to Guyanese communities and assist them in solving economic development challenges. For example, the funds collected could be combined those from other sources to assist with investment in local entrepreneurial cooperatives through a microfinance program that supports market/value chain development.

Microfinance funding can provide individuals and groups with the opportunity to access small loans to start or grow a business. Such loans of a thousand US dollars or less, on average, can be repaid at a manageable negotiable rate. The Diaspora Engagement Network can serve as the conduit for the loan finances, and disperse and manage them through the Diaspora Engagement International Fund. When the loans are repaid, they can be recycled back to the Fund.

By establishing savings groups, The Diaspora Engagement Network can train Guyana community group members to save money on a regular basis. These community groups can be of 20 to 25 members who meet weekly to deposit money into a joint savings account. Once this is established, members can take turns borrowing money for these micro business enterprises.

Instead of operating smaller scale single proprietorship enterprises, many Guyanese business owners want to do more. They would like to meet the market demand for products whether these are crops, locally made clothes, baskets, livestock, computer software or products for bigger and more distant markets. The Diaspora Engagement Network can train farmers and other private business owners to form producer groups, select appropriate products, improve the quality and value of their products, and employ standard metrics to help them negotiate better prices.

Grants

Other funding, such as grants, come with attendant benefits and advantages. Grants, for the purposes of diaspora engagement, could be in the form of cash contributions from a grantor (a government or other sponsor), for a specified purpose to an eligible recipient (called the grantee). Grants are usually conditional upon certain qualifications as to the use, of specified standards, or a proportional contribution by the. Grant writing is the preparation of a funding proposal to access a particular grant. It usually states the purpose of the grant, the steps to be taken to achieve the stated purposes, the budget required for the grant and how the budget is going to be spent. The recipient of the grant is not expected to repay the grant to the grantor.

There are potentially a lot of grants (about 50 million worth from government sources alone) that are available for projects such as diaspora engagement. They are available by application and are awarded every year through foundations, corporate entities and governmental sponsors. Usually nonprofit organizations that are not applying for these available funds are said to be leaving money on the table or passing up money that will eventually be given to other organizations.

Various nonprofits can apply for grants: This includes new nonprofits and those that serve international purposes such as diaspora engagement. Many foundations stand ready to fund nonprofits for development work and for improvement of society in general. For any nonprofit organization to receive grant funding they usually have to complete the meticulous research to identify granting entities, get their attention, develop a relationship and connect with the grantors that are sympathetic to their cause. The latter are willing to fund a variety of needs of nonprofits like the Diaspora Engagement Network. Grants are available for endowment funding, capital campaigns, operational costs, and also for unrestricted purposes. However, successful acquisition of a grant requires the submission of a technically correct proposal of the highest standards usually prepared by a qualified grant writer. To obtain the most out of a typical grant program:

(1) Begin with a diversified strategic fundraising plan. Fundraising authorities recommend that grant awards should not exceed 20% of the funds your nonprofit intends to raise

(2) Commit from the inception to investing the resources and time to researching the foundations, other grant-making entities and opportunities for grant writing on behalf of your organization

(3) Locate a qualified, certified grant writer with the experience of writing winning grants and provide grant writing training for other staff members in the grant writing office

(4) Ensure that your organization matches the stated qualifications for receiving the grant

(5) Ensure that the application is tailored to all the metrics and other requirements required for the grant

(6) Be certain that your application is in alignment for the kinds of funding stated in your fund raising strategic plan

(7) Establish a relationship with the foundation or the (granting agency prior to submitting your proposal first-time applications are rarely funded if unknown to the grantor).

Be aware that grant funding can never serve all your organization's needs. Collateral funding strategies must be in place to provide the essential funding for the operations of your organization.

An office of grant writing and sponsored programs is essential to provide a range of grant services to diaspora team leaders, volunteers and staff for the DEN to seek funding from public and private not-for-profit sponsors. The grant writing staff needs to be trained in grant writing and grant management. Once trained, they can assist diaspora members in navigating through the proposal development, submission, and award set up processes. These grant specialists can help interpret sponsor guidelines and application instructions, assist in budget development, and ensure that applications and incoming awards meet all compliance requirements. The grant writing office can also provide organizational sign off on proposal submissions, accept incoming awards, and negotiate a wide variety of grant-related agreements, including sub-awards to and from sponsors. Initially, this office can be run with grant writing and sponsored programs volunteers in training. In time however, a percentage of grant funding can be devoted to the operational funds needed to sustain the office and its commensurate grant writing services.

Fund raising events

Annual or bi-annual galas, fund raising dinners, masked balls and events such as major gifts, raffles, auctions when taken together form appropriate cornerstone fund raising events for the DEN.

Other events may include limited over cricket games, fund raising soccer games, mystery cruises, dominoes challenges, chess challenge games and others. Funding raising authorities recommend that a committee should be tasked with planning each event. It is important that this committee be formed early in the planning of the event.

The committee will need to start the work at least twelve months prior to the gala and other events. For the purpose of planning a gala or dinner for the DEN, seven to nine persons are recommended. The planning arrangements are very muchthe same for the gala and the dinners. The planning committees for all events may comprise board members as well as diaspora volunteers who can serve as planners as well as workers at the events. Gala and dinner committee members need to be committed to the cause and display a passion for telling others about it. They need to have or develop connections with potential donors and others who can donate items and encourage their colleagues and cohorts to attend the events.

Both the Gala and fund raising dinners should have a theme aligned with the mission of the DEN. Honorees and awards may be presented to influential persons with the highest contributions to the mission of the DEN. This will help to educate the attendees to the cause and work of the DEN. It will also help to motivate and inspire other members in the ranks to devote their maximum time and effort to the work of the DEN. Existing groups with ties to the mission and purposes of the DEN can play a large role in assisting in the planning of fund raising events of the DEN. All Guyana Associations in the region where the DEN is located will be able to identify with the mission, goals and objectives of the DEN and its fund raising activities and are expected to be among its prime supporters.

Timely research is essential when planning a fund raising event like a gala. This research may be focused on the feasibility, of the event, its costs, possible attendance and likelihood of success. Volunteers and others with experience in running comparable events can be invaluable in this respect. Careful consideration needs to be taken in featuring or making commitments to entertainers and celebrities, particularly if this entails exorbitant costs.

Regardless of the event, a pre-requisite is to establish a budget early in the process and keep costs lean. A good place to begin is with the biggest expenses such as the food and beverages (remember to include the wages for bartenders, waiters and caterers). Items often forgotten are rental fees for the venue and advertising costs. Other major costs may include transportation, security, parking, and hotel fees for special guests. Hidden costs are easy to exclude. These often include the time and effort of diaspora volunteers. The venue for the gala should be reserved well in advance of the event. Some locations insist that space be booked for at least six months to a year in advance. This should be done as soon as the planning committee has chosen a date. Securing the venue well in advance would allow other events at the same location to be booked around the date for your gala or dinner.

A good strategy for the gala and dinner planning committees is to ask the owners of the gala venue to donate the space and other event facilities as their donation to the charitable event. The owners of the space are more likely to grant this request if the request for the donation of the space is made far ahead of the event. When the event

venue is a newly opened facility or a historic one, the owners may welcome the opportunity to showcase it and be more willing to donate all or a proportion of it.

The planning committee should seek corporate

sponsorships to help to defray the cost of the gala and dinner. Board members or other diaspora members may have connections that can be useful for identifying sponsors. When this is done, the next step is to be clear to the prospective sponsors about what benefit the sponsor's enterprise will receive for their sponsorship. It is best to limit the number of sponsors to ensure that they get the maximum recognition and exposure for supporting the charitable event. Be careful to delegate tasks in a responsible and intelligent manner.

It is important to delegate tasks to volunteers that are trained or have the skills to complete them successfully. Volunteers are ideal for completing straight forward but important essential tasks such as selling, maintaining mailing lists, selling tickets, stuffing envelopes, checking in arriving guests and the preparation of gift bags. Every opportunity will be used to promote the gala or other charitable event. Free publicity is often available from newspapers, radio and TV stations. In addition, periodic press releases will be publicized and the event will be posted on the DEN's website. Invitations leaders will be sent to well wishers, and supporters, community and others most interested in the DEN and its associated charitable events.

Bibliography

"Actividad Economica, Migracion a Estados Unidos Y Remesas   En   El Occidente de Mexico." *Migraciones Internacionales* 2, no. 1 (n.d.): 136–58. Print

Adams, R.H. Jr. "Remittances, Investment, and Rural Asset Accumulation in Pakistan." *Economic Development and Cultural Change* 47, no. 1 (2002): 155–73.

Arroyo, Alejandre, and Valenzuela, Corvera. "Efectos Subregionales de Las Remesas de Emigrantes Mixicanos En Estados Unidos." *Comercio Exterior* 50, no. 4 (2003): 340–49.

Bach, S. "International Migration of Health Workers: Labour and Social Issues." *Working Paper, 209.* Geneva: ILO, 2003.

Ballard, R. "Remittances and Economic Development in India and Pakistan." In *Remittances: Development Impact and Future Prospects.* Washington, D.C.: World Bank, 2000.

Binford, L. "Mexican Seasonal Migration to Canada and Development: A Community-Based Comparison." *International Migration* 41, no. 2 (2003): 3–26.

Brinkerhoff, Jennifer. *Diasporas and Development: Exploring the Potential.* Boulder, Co: Rinner Publishers, 2008.

Browne, Stephen. *Aid and Influence: Do Donors Help or Hinder?* London: Earthscan Publishers, 2007.

Cohen, J, Jones R., and Conway, D. "Migrant Remittances and (Under)Development in Mexico." *Critique of Anthropology* 23, no. 3 (n.d.): 305–36.

Garza, R, and Lowell, B. L. "The Development of the Hometown Associations in the United States and the Use of Social Remittances in Mexico." In *Sending Money Home: Hispanic Remittance and Community Development*. Lanham, MD: Rowman & Littlefield, n.d.

Kingman, Mireille. *Nurses on the Move: Migration and the Global Health Care Economy*. New York: Cornell University Press, 2006.

Mercer, Claire, Page Ben, and Evans, Martin. *Development and the African Diaspora*. London: Zed Books, 2008.

Mertz, Barbara, Chen Lincoln, and Geithner, Peter. *Diasporas and Development*. Boston: Harvard University Press, 2007.

"Migration of Mexican Seasonal Farm Workers to Canada and Development: Obstacles to Productive Investment." *International Migration Review* 34, no. 1 (2003): 79–97.

APPENDIX A.

Sponsors of Charitable International Projects

United States Agency for International Development (USAID)
Information Center
USAID, Ronald Reagan Building, Washington, D.C. 20523-1000
Phone: (202) 712-4810 Email: pinquiries@usaid.gov - Web:
www.USAID.GOV

Some USAID Funded Projects

American Schools & Hospitals Abroad (ASHA)
The Office of American Schools and Hospitals Abroad provides
grants to competitively selected private, non-profit universities
and secondary schools, libraries, and medical centers abroad.
Since the inception of the program, ASHA has assisted 257
institutions in over 76 countries, and facilitated the development
and sustainment of superior libraries, schools, and medical
centers, positively impacting the regions where these institutions
are located.

Child Survival & Health Programs

The Child Survival and Health Grants Programs (CSHGP)
promotes a unique and productive partnership with U.S. private
voluntary (PVOs) and non-profit
Organizations and their in-country partners. The program
supports effective community-based maternal and child health
programs that contribute to reducing infant, child, maternal and

infectious disease-related mortality and morbidity in developing countries.

PVOs and their local partners provide high quality, sustainable child survival and health interventions in a variety of program settings, from the smallest, most remote communities to large, district- wide programs, partnering with community groups and district and national health authorities.

The Denton Transportation Program

The Denton Program allows private U.S. citizens and U.S. based non-governmental organizations to use space available on U.S. military cargo planes to transport humanitarian items such as clothing, food, medical and educational supplies, agricultural equipment and vehicles to countries in need. The program is jointly administered by USAID, the Department of State (DOS), and the Department of Defense (DoD). In FY 2003, over 300,000 pounds of humanitarian goods were sent to seven countries through the Denton program.

DIV Development Innovation Ventures

USAID launched Development Innovation Ventures (DIV) as a way of producing development outcomes more effectively and cost-efficiently while managing risk and obtaining leverage. Through DIV, USAID seeks to identify and rigorously test promising projects with the potential to significantly (rather than incrementally) improve development outcomes, and help replicate and scale projects that are proven successful. DIV expects its most successful of investments will have an accelerated growth path to reach tens of millions of beneficiaries worldwide within 10 years.

Food for Peace

USAID, through funding provided by Public Law 480, Title II, makes commodity donations to Cooperating Sponsors (Private Voluntary Organizations, Cooperatives, and International Organization Agencies) to address the needs of food security in both 5-year development projects and emergency food assistance programs. Food for Peace provides assistance primarily through its various programs:

Grand Challenges

USAID has defined Grand Challenges for Development to focus global attention on specific development outcomes based on transformational, scalable, and sustainable change. Grand Challenge in Development is a way to describe a large and solvable problem. It is not just a statement of a problem, but a definable, and quantifiable goal, that can be achieved over a specified time frame. The goal itself defines the outcomes by which success is measured.

GDA Global Development Alliance

The Global Development Alliance is an innovative public-private alliance model for improving social and economic conditions in developing countries. It combines the assets and experience of strategic partners, leveraging their capital and investments, creativity, and access to markets, to solve complex problems facing government, business, and communities. Through 2006, USAID had put together more than 600 public-private partnerships, committing $1.5 billion and leveraging $4.8 billion of partner resources.

Limited Excess Property Program

Through the Limited Excess Property Program (LEPP), Private Voluntary Organizations (PVOs) can acquire U.S. government excess property for use in their programs and projects overseas. To participate they must be registered with United States Agency for International Development (USAID) and take the equipment on an as is, where is basis. Through LEPP, USAID makes it possible for millions of dollars of excess property to be utilized in dozens of developing countries.

Localworks

Localworks is an opportunity to promote the capacity for locally-owned and led development by strengthening networks of local development actors and increasing access to local resources. At least three Missions will be competitively selected to implement a multi-year *localworks* program. Missions will receive specialized financial, technical, and human resource support to help create bridges between key local actors. The program is open to all sectors and regions.

Ocean Freight Reimbursement

The Ocean Freight Reimbursement (OFR) Program provides small competitive grants to approximately 50 U.S. Private Voluntary Organizations (PVOs) each year, allowing recipients to ship a wide variety of goods overseas for use in privately funded development and humanitarian assistance programs. Funds are used to reimburse the PVOs' costs to transport donated commodities, such as medical or educational supplies, agricultural equipment and construction equipment to developing countries. OFR is on a two-year cycle so Requests for Applications (RFAs) are released (bi-annually). The Program reaches out to small and/or newly registered PVOs by providing grants to many first-time applicants.

International Diaspora Engagement Alliance

c/o Migration Policy Institute

1400 16th Street NW, Suite 300

Washington, D.C. 20036-2257

Tel: 202-266-1940

Email: info@diasporaalliance.org

Web: www.diasporaalliance.org

United States Agency for International Development (USAID)

Information Center: USAID, Ronald Reagan Building, Washington, D.C. 20523-1000

Phone: (202) 712-4810

Email: pinquiries@usaid.gov

Web: www.usaid.gov

World Bank Headquarters

1818 H Street, NW
Washington, DC 20433 USA

Tel: (202) 473-1000
Fax: (202) 477-6391

Web: worldbank.org

African Diaspora Program

Web: worldbank.org/afr/diaspora

Email: afrdiaspora@worldbank.org

Global Forum for Migration and Development, International, gfmd.org: An annual meeting that convenes policy makers, high-level practitioners, and other stakeholders from UN member states to discuss policies, challenges, opportunities, and best practices in migration and development. Their website is a good source of information about national migration and development policies.

International Labor Organization (ILO), International, ilo.org: UN organization that works to promote social justice by encouraging decent employment opportunities and protecting workers rights. Involved in implementing the UN-EU Joint Migration and Development Initiative.

IDEA, 2012-last update, 2012 Global Diaspora Forum: Moving Forward by Going Back [Homepage of International Diaspora Engagement Alliance], [Online].

At at Website: http://diasporaalliance.org/featured/global-diaspora-forum/ [Nov 18, 2012].

United Nations Development Program (UNDP), the World Health Organization (WHO), United Nations International Children's Emergency Fund (UNICEF), Food and Agriculture Organization (FAO), and World Food Program. Multilateral agencies that deal primarily in financial resource transfer, including the World Bank (International Development Agency and International Bank for Reconstruction and Development), and the Foundation for Agricultural Development. Other groups include the Consultative Group on International Agricultural Research consortium and others dealing with specialized developmental issues and problems. Among these is the Swedish Agency for Research Cooperation with Developing Countries, the International Development Research Centre of Canada, and the Australian Development Assistance Bureau. The assistance of these public agencies may be complimented by the private efforts of foundations, international voluntary agencies, and other institutions. Major private American foundations engaged in development work include foundations like are Ford, Rockefeller, and Carnegie; and several new foundations emerging in the United States, Europe, and Japan. Some of the most visible are international voluntary agencies such as CARE, Catholic Relief Services, and Oxfam. These public and private agencies are often enjoined with research universities conducting research in disciplinary fields including nutrition-related fields of public health, agriculture, economics, and management.

Appendix B.

Guyana Diaspora Needs Assessment/Survey

Kindly fill in the correct response.

Q 1. NAME	First Name	
	Middle Name	
	Surname	
Q 2. GENDER	Male	
	Female	
Q3. AGE	> 18	
	50–59	
	19–29	
	30–39	
	40–49	
	> 59	

Q 4. MARITAL STATUS	Marital Status	Single	
		Married	
		Divorced	
		Widowed	
Q 5. CHILDREN	How many Children do you have?	0	
		1	
		2	
		3	
		4	
		>5	
Q 6. EDUCATION	What is the highest level of education you have reached?	Primary	
		High School (Secondary)	
		University or College	
		University (bachelor's degree)	
		University (Master's degree)	
		University (Ph.D. degree)	

Q 7. What is your profession? (Circle your profession)	
Administration	Accounting/Finance/Banking
Media/advertising/ entertainment	Sales/marketing
Finance/banking	Science/research
Customer services	Sport/ health/cosmetology
Community services	Sales/marketing
Construction	Transport/logistics
Consulting /corporate strategy	Retail/consumer industry
Education/training	Engineering
Government	Health care/medical
Hospitality/tourism	HR/ Recruitment
IT/technology	Other, please specify
Insurance/legal	
Manufacturing	
Mining/environmental resource	

Q 8. WHAT IS YOUR AVERAGE ANNUAL INCOME? CIRCLE THE CORECT RESPONSE
No income
< US $10,000
$10,000–$20,000
$20,000–$30,000
$30,000–$40,000
$40,000-50,000
$50,000–$70,000
$70,000–$100,000
>$100,000
No response

Q 9. In What country were you born?
Guyana
USA (To Guyanese parents or otherwise)
Canada (To Guyanese parents or otherwise)
UK (To Guyanese parents or otherwise)
Other, please specify:

Q10. WHAT IS YOUR CURRENT NATIONALITY?
US Citizen?
Canadian Citizen?
British Citizen?
Dual Citizenship (Please specify)
Other Citizenship (Please specify)

Q11.   In what country do you currently live?
The United States of America (US
United Kingdom (UK)
Canada
Other Caribbean Country
Europe
Other (Please specify)

Q12. WHEN DID YOU LEAVE GUYANA TO RESIDE IN THE DIASPORA?
The United States of America (US)
United Kingdom (UK)
Canada
Other Caribbean Country
Europe
Other (Please specify)

Q13. WHAT WAS YOUR PRIMARY REASON FOR LEAVING GUYANA?
To pursue further education
To pursue better Employment opportunities
To open a business abroad
I moved with my family as a child or a dependent
Because of my marriage to someone living in the diaspora
For political/asylum
Other (Please specify)

Q 14. IF YOU ARE MARRIED WITH A LONG-TERM PARTNER, WHAT IS THE NATIONALITY OF YOUR SPOUSE/LONG-TERM PARTNER?
Guyanese Citizen?
US Citizen?
UK Citizen?
Canadian Citizen?
Other Caribbean country? (Please specify)
Other? (Please specify)

Q15. ARE ANY OF YOUR IMMEDIATE FAMILY MEMBERS (SPOUSE, CHILDREN, PARENTS) WITH YOU IN THE COUNTRY IN WHICH YOU CURRENTLY LIVE?
No
Yes – Spouse
Yes – Children
Yes – Parents
Other (Please specify)

Q16. ARE ANY OF YOUR IMMEDIATE FAMILY MEMBERS (SPOUSE, CHILDREN, PARENTS) STILL IN GUYANA?
No
Yes - Spouse
Yes - Children
Yes - Parents
Other

Q17. IS DUAL CITIZENSHIP AN ATTRACTIVE OPTION FOR YOU?
Yes
No
Of no Interest

Q 18. ON AVERAGE, HOW OFTEN DO YOU RETURN TO GUYANA?
Once every two years
Once every three years
Never
Other (Please specify)

Q19. ON AVERAGE, HOW LONG DO YOU STAY WHEN YOU VISIT GUYANA?
Less than 1 week
1–2 weeks
2–4 weeks
1 –2 months
3–6 months
6 months–1year
More than 1year
Other (Please specify)

Q20. FOR WHAT PURPOSES DO YOU VISIT GUYANA?
Holiday
To visit friends and family
For Business
For Educational purposes
Other, (Please specify)

Q21. DO YOU EXPECT O RETURN TO GUYANA IN THE FUTURE PERMANENTLY? HOW SOON?
Yes
No
Not sure
In the next six months

Q21. DO YOU EXPECT O RETURN TO GUYANA IN THE FUTURE PERMANENTLY? HOW SOON?
Yes
No
Not sure
In the next six months

Q22. If yes, how soon do you expect to return?
In 6 months to 1 year
In 1–2 years
In 2–5 years
In more than 5 years
Not sure

Q23. ARE THERE ANY BARRIERS TO YOUR RETURN?
No
Not sure?
Financial constraints?
Other, (Please specify)

Q 24. IF YES, WHAT ARE THE BARRIERS TO YOUR RETURN?
Work commitments
Accommodation/housing
Political/legal
Other, please specify
Yes
Q25. WOULD YOU BE INTERESTED IN RETURNING TO GUYANA TEMPORARILY AS PART OF A "SKILLS TRANSFER" PROGRAM?
No
Not sure
Less than 2 weeks
Other, please specify

Q26. IF YES, HOW MUCH TIME WOULD YOU BE WILLING TO SPEND IN GUYANA ON A "SKILLS TRANSFER" PROGRAM?
2 weeks to a month
1–2 months
3–6 months
7–12 months
More than a year
Not sure
Telephone
Q27. HOW DO YOU MAINTAIN CONTACT WITH FRIENDS AND FAMILY IN GUYANA?
E-mails
Twitter
Facebook
Letters
Word of mouth
Newspapers
Other, please specify

Q28. SINCE BEING IN THE COUNTRY OF YOUR CURRENT RESIDENCE, HAVE YOU EVER SENT FINANCES TO FAMILY MEMBERS OR FRIENDS IN GUYANA?
[ ] Yes,   [ ] No

Q29. SINCE BEING IN THE COUNTRY OF YOUR CURRENT RESIDENCE, HAVE YOU EVER SENT FINANCES TO FAMILY MEMBERS OR FRIENDS IN GUYANA?
[ ] Yes,   [ ] No

Q 30. HOW MUCH DO YOU SEND ON AVERAGE PER TRANSACTION?
Kindly circle the correct amounts
< US $100
US $100–300
US $300–500
US $500–1,000
US $1,000–2,500
US $2,500–5,000
US $5,000–10,000
>US10,000
Other please specify

Q31. HOW DO YOU REMIT FUNDS TO GUYANA?
Western Union
MoneyGram
Quick pay

Q 32. WHAT IS THE AVERAGE COST OF SENDING FINANCES?
US $1
US $1-$5
US $6-$10
US $11-$25
US $26-$50
US $51-$100
>$100
Other, Specify

Q 33. WHY DO YOU SEND FINANCES TO GUYANA? CIRCLE ALL THAT APPLY
Financial support for family or friends
Contributions for development projects
Personal investment
Debt service
Personal obligation
Other, please specify

Q 34.WHAT IS THE AVERAGE COST OF SENDING FINANCES?
US $1
US $1-$5
US $6-$10
US $11-$25
US $26-$50
US $51-$100
>$100
Other, Specify

Q35. DO YOU BELIEVE THE FINANCES SENT CONTRIBUTE TO THE DEVELOPMENT OF THE FOLLOWING? (CIRCLE ALL THAT APPLY)
Education
Health care provision
Infrastructure development
Churches or faith-based organizations
Women's associations
Childcare
Other areas of development (specify)

Q 36. DO YOU HAVE ANY PROPERTIES/ ASSETS IN GUYANA?	
[ ] Yes	[ ] No
Q37. Do you have any private investments in Guyana?	
[ ] Yes	[ ] No
Q38. ARE YOU INTERESTED IN PRIVATE INVESTMENT IN GUYANA?	
[ ] Yes [ ] No [ ] Not sure	

Q 39. IF YES, WHAT TYPE OF INVESTMENT WOULD BE OF INTEREST TO YOU? (CRCLE ALL THAT APPLY)
Manufacturing
Financial services
Agriculture/horticulture
Transport
Mining
Tourism
Import-Export
Other, please specify

Q 40. ARE YOU CURRENTLY INTERESTED IN CONTRIBUTING OR DONATING TO DEVELOPMENT PROJECTS IN GUYANA?
[ ] Yes   [ ] No.   [ ] Not sure
Q 41. WHAT TYPES OF DEVELOPMENT PROJECTS ARE YOU INTERESTED IN SUPPORTING? (CIRCLE ALL THAT APPLY)
Education
Health care provision or Childcare
Infrastructure development
Microfinance initiatives
Churches or faith-based organizations
Women's associations

Q 42. What type of support can you contribute? (Circle all that apply)
Financial
Material
Skills transfer
Other, please specify
Financial
Material
Skills transfer
Other, please specify
Georgetown (and Greater Georgetown)
Linden
New Amsterdam
East Coast (Specify Demerara or Berbice)
West Coast (Specify Demerara or Berbice)
Skeldon
Bartica
Others, please specify

Q 43. WHICH PARTS OF GUYANA WOULD YOU BE INTERESTED IN HELPING TO DEVELOP? (SPECIFY ALL THAT APPLY)
Georgetown (and Greater Georgetown)
Linden
New Amsterdam
East Coast (Specify Demarara or Berbice)
West Coast (Specify Demarara or Berbice)
Skeldon
Bartica
Others, please specify

Q 44. ARE THERE ANY BARRIERS OR RESTRICTIONS THAT EXIST THAT COULD STOP YOU FROM CONTRIBUTING TO NATIONAL DEVELOPMENT?
Yes
No
Not sure
Other, Specify

Q 45. IF YES, WHAT ARE THESE BARRIERS? CIRCLE ALL THAT APPLY)	
Financial constraints	
Work commitments	
Political/legal	
Other, please specify	

Q 44. DO YOU BELONG TO A DIASPORA NETWORK (FORMAL OR INFORMAL)? (CIRCLE ALL THAT APPLY)	
No	Academic Work-based
Guyana Association	Internet-based social networking
Collaborating groups	Other, please specify

Q 45. HOW IS INFORMATION SHARED AMONG MEMBERS OF THE DIASPORA? (SPECIFY ALL THAT APPLY)	
Meetings	
E-mails	
Websites	
Twitter	
Facebook	
Newsletters	
Word of mouth	
Other, please specify	

Q 46. How often do you meet? Kindly Circle the correct response	
Every two weeks	Every six months
Monthly	Yearly
Fortnightly	Other, please specify
Quarterly	

Q 47. Is there a contact person/ focal point for your diaspora network?
[ ] Yes   [ ] No

Q 48. If yes, specify details	
Name (specify)	Phone number (specify)
Address (specify)	E-mail

Q 49. Would you be interested in receiving additional information about projects for Guyanese diaspora in the future? - If yes, please indicate your e-mail address
[ ] Yes   [ ] No

Q 50. Would you be willing for us to contact you to provide additional information on the above questions? If yes, please indicate your e-mail address
[ ] Email Address   Phone:

Q 51. What is your preferred method of communication
Phone: Email: Other, Please specify

Appendix B (cont'd)

Interview Schedules

I. Interview Questions and Guidelines
II. Interview with Interview with diaspora associations in the US

I. Questions and answers

1.a) How many diaspora associations are there in the USA?
b) Which ones are the main ones?

2. What activities/services are they engaged in?

3. What resources are there in the diaspora that may contribute to Guyanese development efforts?

4. Are there any development and investment/trade initiatives in Guyana driven by the Guyana High Commission in the US?
(Please describe any efforts to encourage the diaspora to return to participate in development initiatives).

5. Are there any development and investment initiatives/activities in Guyana driven by the diaspora?

6. What are the major challenges faced by the diaspora in terms of participating in development efforts in Guyana?

7. What are the major constraints related to engaging the diaspora in national development?

8. What strategies are/can be used for engaging the diaspora in national development?

9. What are the major challenges the diaspora face in their bid to return home?

9. What would the diaspora like to see changed or addressed to help with their long- and short-term return plans to participate in national development?

10. Please state any issues you would like addressed by current diaspora engagement strategies?

11. Is there a compelling rationale for diaspora engagement in the development of Guyana?

Interview with diaspora associations in the US

1. What are the main activities of your association?

2. How many members do you have?

3. How do you do your networking and what challenges do you face in that regard?

4. What skills and resources are available in your membership? Profile of members.

5. Is the association or any of its members involved in any development and investment/trade initiatives in Guyana? If yes, what are they?

6. What constraints exist in engaging the members in development activities in Guyana?

7. Are there members who wish to return to Guyana on a short-term or long-term basis? If so, what are the major challenges they face in this regard?

8. Would you participate in an initiative to encourage your members to return to Guyana on a long-term or short-term basis?

9. What measures would encourage members to engage in investment/trade or development activities in Guyana?

10. Are there any areas in which the diaspora have expressed interest in terms of investment in Guyana?

11. Please state any issue you would like addressed in a diaspora engagement initiative.

12. Is there a compelling rationale for diaspora engagement in the homeland of Guyana?

APPENDIX C

Diasporas for Development Resource Guide

(Reprinted here with permission of Dr. Joyce Millen at Willamette University, USA)

Written by Claire Hoffman and members of the ISA-CGC

Guide also available at:

http://www.willamette.edu/dept/isa-cgc/index.html

Contact:

Institute for the Social Analysis of Complex Global Challenges,

- Willamette University
  900 State Street jmillen@willamette.edu
  503.370.6593
- National Science Foundation Institute for the Social Analysis:
  Willamette University of Complex Global Challenges

RESOURCE GUIDE

Lessons learned

This resource guide is intended to aid members of the African Diaspora in their efforts to bring resources and skills to their home communities in Africa. It was prepared in collaboration with scholars, healthcare practitioners, and members of the Africa diaspora.

The international community is increasingly recognizing the important role diaspora communities play in the development of their countries of origin, and a growing number of organizations are seeking to encourage and build upon diaspora-led development initiatives. While this trend is reflected in a growing body of literature and several high-level conferences dedicated to the field of migration and development. it is clear that more needs to be done to make information and resources more accessible to diaspora members working at the grassroots level. Though far from comprehensive, this guide seeks to address this issue by profiling organizations that exemplify the types and sources of support available to diaspora development actors.

Though the idea of development through migration did not fully emerge on the international agenda until the late 1990s, early programs linking the two were established as early as the 1970s. Pioneers included the United Nations Development Program (UNDP), France, and the Netherlands (de Haas 2006). The UNDP's TOKTEN program values the transnational identities of migrants and promotes development through circular migration. In contrast, early French codevelopment programs and the REMPLOD project

in the Netherlands focused primarily on encouraging and

facilitating return migration. These early programs achieved little credibility or success and have since been disbanded or restructured (de Haas 2006).

The extraordinary impact of migrant remittances on the economies of their countries of origin. This in turn led to more research, conferences, and even some concrete action seeking to leverage diaspora communities for the development of their communities and countries of origin. Today, though only a select few organizations implement programs that specifically target diaspora individuals and associations, diaspora members are now widely recognized as strategic and important agents of development.

For members of the African diaspora who are looking for resources to realize their development goals, this means that an unparalleled number of organizations are currently open to the prospect of supporting diaspora-led development initiatives. As this field is relatively new, however, many programs and policies are exploratory and transient. A large number are active for approximately three years at a time, followed by a period of evaluation to determine their effectiveness before funding for a second phase can be secured. Currently, much of the dialog and action among practitioners of migration and development centers on identifying and sharing best practices and conditions for success. This knowledge will hopefully translate into more sustained sources of support in the future. With the exception of organizations devoted entirely to diaspora development work, windows of opportunity to access the resources of many organizations can be of relatively short duration.

This field is also characterized by an extensive amount of inter-organizational and international collaboration, which is reflected in the vast and complex web of funding and implementing partnership that join together to generate and implement programs. For ease of navigation, we have rather artificially untangled this web to place programs under the entry for one organization. In reality, most programs are the result of funding and work contributed by several organizational partners. For example, the Africa-Europe Platform (AEP), a network that aims to connect African diaspora organizations and stakeholders throughout the European Union, is managed and funded by a combination of 10 different organizations.

Many programs are established via a top-down approach involving organizations at a variety of different levels. National policies and approaches regarding migration and development are often the result of, or influenced by international conferences and forums such as the Global Forum for Migration and Development (GFMD). As public institutions are a major source of funding and technical support, these national policies hold significant influence over the actions taken by private organizations. In several countries, networks of diaspora members have played an active role in establishing programs from the bottom up by successfully lobbying for institutional support and funding. In either case, most of the organizations profiled in this guide are either part of or receive funding from the national government in their respective country, and often receive support from one or more international or regional organizations as well.

To accommodate the diverse ways in which diaspora members act in solidarity with their countries of origin, we chose to profile organizations whose programs reflect the variety of resources available to diaspora communities. While each organization's programs are unique, reflecting their particular priorities and strengths, it is possible to organize the resources provided by traditional development actors. These categories are by no means exclusive—the resources provided by many of the programs in this guide could fall under multiple categories—but meant to give a general overview of the resources available.

- **Funding and capacity building for diaspora organizations:** Recognizing the value of diaspora organizations as development actors and advocates, many organizations seek to build up the initiatives of diaspora organizations through capacity building and grants. This diverse array of resources includes grants that can be used to research, plan, and implement a development project or establish services and programs, usually in partnership with a local organization in the country of origin. Capacity building services include workshops, conferences, and personalized training in areas such as strategic planning, fundraising and financial management or can include services like website hosting facilities.

- **Facilitating skills transfer:** These programs encourage circular migration by facilitating opportunities for diaspora members to employ their skills and expertise through consultancies or volunteer placements in their countries of origin. Typically, these programs recruit highly skilled and experienced volunteers to address particular shortages in human resources, often in the areas of education, health, agriculture, and business. Most also require that volunteers work exclusively in their country of origin.

- **Facilitating remittances and investment:** In response to data demonstrating the importance of remittances to the economies of countries of origin, some institutions seek to maximize their economic potential by making the remittance transfer market more transparent, effective, and less costly. Some organizations also seek to create incentives to encourage diaspora members to channel their funds into productive investments. These include programs in which remitting diaspora members receive tax deductions or receive co-financing on philanthropic investments.

  - **Promoting and equipping entrepreneurship:** These programs seek to increase capital investment and sources of sustainable livelihoods in diaspora members' countries of origin by equipping entrepreneurs to establish businesses or expand existing businesses into their countries of origin. funding and technical assistance through highly competitive business contests. Other programs avoid providing funding, but provide training and resources for motivated entrepreneurs with various levels of expertise to access the credit they need and implement a successful business.

- **Creating venues for networking, lobbying and advocacy:** Many organizations seek to create networks of diaspora organizations and other stakeholders to serve as vehicles for resource consolidation, partnership formation, knowledge sharing, and advocacy. Members of these networks typically include diaspora organizations, government representatives, and other non-governmental actors interested in supporting the work of diaspora organizations

- **Multilateral Organizations:** International organizations play a highly influential and important role in developing, implementing, and funding policies and programs that link migration and development work. By providing an international venue for circulating knowledge and creating partnerships, the GMFD, for example, has significant influence on programs implemented at all levels. Some organizations, like the IOM and the UNDP, implement their own programs to facilitate skill and resource transfers, while others, most notably the EU, are vital sources of funding for programs implemented at the national and private level.

- **National Institutions:** National development institutions are particularly influential in efforts to establish networks of diaspora members, co-finance development projects, and facilitate remittance transfers. The governments of France, Belgium, and the UK have established national platforms that promote diaspora-led development and advocacy by linking diaspora organizations with resources, other stakeholders, and policymakers. For the most part, national programs that engage diaspora members directly are implemented through public-private partnerships with local NGOs.

- **Private Nonprofits/NGOs:** Private nonprofit organizations play an instrumental role in implementing programs to equip diaspora development actors, either on their own, with other nonprofits, or in partnership with public institutions. In this category, we include more traditional development actors who work with diaspora members, as well as diaspora-led organizations like AFFORD and ERCMOVE that seek to enhance the development contributions of diaspora members from multiple countries.

The MacArthur Foundation, and the Hand Foundation that support diaspora-led initiatives indirectly by funding organizations that engage with diaspora communities, such as the International Diaspora Engagement Alliance (IdEA) and the African Diaspora Policy Center (ADPC). The second are foundations that fund grassroots development projects, but have not demonstrated a particular commitment to the work of diaspora organizations. Information about some of these foundations can be found in the Additional Resources section of this guide.

Trade Organizations: International and national trade organizations like the International Nursing Association and the American Medical Association are potential sources of equipment, professional expertise, and other resources for international development projects. While we did not find a trade organization that reaches out to diaspora professionals in particular, these are important networks that can and have been leveraged for resources such as medical equipment, and others.

Banks: Not surprisingly, banks are key partners in international efforts to facilitate the transfer of remittances. Many development agencies, including USAID, UK DFID, the French Ministry of Foreign Affairs, and the World Bank, are working with banks to help develop remittance transfer services that are faster, cheaper, easier to use, and can transfer funds to more places. Certain banks are getting involved at a deeper level to support the economic

initiatives of diaspora members, co-finance development projects, and facilitate diaspora-led research and action pertaining to improving remittance transfers.

Faith-Based Organizations: This category includes individual and networks of churches, mosques, synagogues, etc. While these organizations may not have a specifically development-related agenda, they often possess significant amounts of human and financial resources that diaspora members belonging to these organizations can tap into to find support for their work.

Research Process

This guide is the culmination of six months of research conducted from May-November 2012. The first phase consisted of generating a snowball sample of approximately 250 organizations potentially involved with diaspora development work. Organizations were identified through "brainstorming" sessions with other contributors to this book, a study of the relevant literature, and by exploring the websites and partner organizations of previously identified organizations. Once an organization was identified as a potential candidate for inclusion, we conducted thorough research on their websites to determine whether they offered resources specifically for diaspora members and organizations and how to access these resources. To make the sample more representative of the many countries involved in diaspora engagement work, online searches for programs in particular countries were conducted on internet-wide search engines and on the websites of national institutions for international development. We also drew from our personal networks and online resources to determine the involvement of certain types of organizations whose work was less visible, including cases, organizations were contacted by phone and email if necessary information could not be located online and/or to confirm that the information found on their website was accurate and up-to-date.

Criteria for Inclusion

The organizations involved in supporting diaspora-led development work are active throughout the globe in both home and host countries. For the purposes of this guide, we chose to profile organizations that seek to mobilize and equip African diaspora development actors living in North America and Europe, as these regions have some of the largest and most established populations of African diaspora members. We also focused on organizations with the capacity and mission to support members of diasporas from multiple African countries. Thus, we have excluded individual diaspora organizations representing a single country or region, as well as governments and other institutions in countries of origin seeking to engage their own diasporas. Organizations were also selected based upon whether they offered concrete programs and resources explicitly for diaspora development actors, and, in some cases, were chosen to provide examples of best practices worthy of emulating. Though our intention was to create a somewhat representational sample of the many countries and types of organizations involved in this work, this guide is heavily influenced by organizations in the Netherlands, France, and the UK. These countries were some of the first to implement migration and development initiatives, presumably as a result of substantial and well-established diaspora communities, and therefore have some of the most developed networks of support organizations.

How to Use This Guide

Organization profiles have been arranged in alphabetical order for ease of navigation. To make it possible to search for organizations

based upon country and/or type of support, we have included a chart at the beginning of this guide that lists each organization, their country location, and the types of resources they provide according to the categories listed above. Each organization profile contains a brief summary highlighting the organization's history, purpose, and impact, as well as information on the resources they provide and how they can be accessed.

Readers of this guide should be aware that the information in these profiles is drawn primarily from the websites of the organizations themselves. While we have tried to ensure that this information is as accurate and up-to-date as possible by contacting organizations via phone and email, we did not receive responses in all cases. Potential sources of support based upon past (and sometimes current) initiatives, so parties interested in a particular organization should visit that organization's website to research current opportunities.

ORGANIZATION PROFILES

1. Africa-Europe Platform (AEP)
African Diaspora Policy Center

Zeestraat 100, 2518 AD, The Hague, the Netherlands

Email: info@ae-platform.org

Web: www.ae-platform.org

Launched in 2011, the goal of this initiative is to create a platform to support the work of African diaspora organizations throughout the 27 EU member states, Switzerland, and Norway **(AEP)**. The goal of this platform is to facilitate greater coordination and communication between African diaspora organizations and connections with other stakeholders and sources of support, such as policymakers and organizations like the African Union. It also aims to equip African diaspora led development through e-learning, trainings, and workshops that are generated by and tailored to the needs of the platform's members. While this platform is funded primarily by the EU and implemented by the ADPC, AFFORD, CGMD, FORIM, and the ICMPD, small diaspora organizations working at the grassroots level have played a very active role in its formation (**AEP**). Through online questionnaires, called e-consultations, members of African diaspora organizations participated in defining the principles and framework of the platform. They are also using e-consultations to collect information about good practices. The results of these e-consultations are published on the AEP website and discussed at "expert meetings," which bring together stakeholders including representatives of African diaspora organizations, representatives of support organizations, and government officials. The first two expert meetings occurred in March and November 2012 and the third will take place in 2013 to reflect on and establish a plan for the platform once it is fully operational (**AEP**).

Resources:

- e-Newsletters: Published 3-4 times per year, these newsletters keep members updated on the platform's activities and other relevant news for African diaspora members in Europe
- e-Policy Briefs: These are published several times per year to inform African diaspora members about key migration and
- Catalogue of Good Practices: Based upon e-consultations, discussions at the 2nd expert meeting, information uploaded onto the AEP website, and feedback from pilot activities. It will provide African diaspora organizations with a series of tools and methods for engaging in development work and will function as a learning tool for stakeholders and policymakers.

Workshops and Trainings: These events provide tailor-made capacity building services that respond to the needs an desires of the platform's members. Event Calendar: offers information about events held throughout Europe that are relevant to the

African diaspora and development issues and present the views of African diaspora members to policymakers and other stakeholders.

E-Learning Courses: To build the capacities of diaspora organizations, these courses address topics such as networking, alliance building, policy engagement, and advocacy. The first e-learning course on networking, alliance-building and policy engagement is available on the AFFORD Institute's website (www.affordinstitute.org) migration and development work.

- Country Profiles: The AEP is in the process of creating profiles for the 29 countries represented by the platform. Each profile contains information about migration demographics, the level of networking among African diaspora organizations, local institutions and organizations that support African diaspora development cooperation, a list of African diaspora associations, and good practices conducted by African diaspora organizations in that country.

Eligibility: Members of African diaspora associations that are active in development cooperation and based out of the 27 EU member states, Switzerland, or Norway are invited to become members of the platform. All materials are available in English and French.

Getting Involved: To register as a member of the AEP platform, members of African diaspora organizations can fill out the registration form on the AEP website (www.ae-platform.org). Information about events and resources sponsored by the AEP can be found on their website or on the websites of its implementing organizations.

The African Development Bank (AfDB): Migration and Development Initiative.

AfDB Temporary Relocation Agency (Tunis)

15 Avenue du Ghana
P.O.Box 323-1002
Tunis-Belvedère, Tunisia
Tel: (+216) 71 10 39 00/(+216) 71 35 19 33
Email: afdb@afdb.org Web: afdb.org

In 1964, 23 newly independent African nations founded the African Development Bank to "contribute to the sustainable economic development and social progress of African countries" (AfDB 2012). Since launching the Migration and Development Initiative in 2009, the AfDB has played a major role in efforts to maximize the development impact of remittances. A 2007 AfDB study conducted in the Comoros, Mali, Morroco, and Senegal found that remittances represent between 9 and 24% of GDP and between 80 and 750% of Official Development Assistance. This study also found that the impact of these remittances is limited by high transfer costs (AfDB 2012). For this reason, the AfDB is generating research and working with other financial institutions to make formal remittance transfer services cheaper and more effective. They also seek to create financial products that are more responsive to the needs of diaspora members, promote the use of formal transfer mechanisms (such as banks), and/or provide incentives for channeling funds into productive investments. To promote local and diaspora-led initiatives that forward these goals, the AfDB established the Migration and Development Trust Fund with support from France and the International Fund for Agricultural Development. Through this fund, the AfDB aims to support projects that do one of the following: enhance knowledge of remittance flows, reduce transfer costs, generate productive investment, or contribute to local development (AfDB 2012). Thus far, the AfDB has issued two calls for proposals that closed in January 2011 and May 2012 (AfDB 2010).

Resources/Initiatives:

Development Marketplace for African Diaspora Action (DMADA):

This initiative aims to support members of the African diaspora who have ideas for innovative and sustainable initiatives that will promote youth employment. Members of diasporas from any country within the AU and living in any region of the world will be eligible to apply through a legally registered organization. The World Bank will release a call for proposals once funding has been confirmed (World Bank 2011).

African Diaspora Professional Skills Database:

ADPSD - Launched in 2010, this initiative seeks to mobilize human resources in the diaspora by creating a database of available skills and resources. This information will be used by World Bank Task Team Leaders to identify individuals and organizations/firms that could contribute to World Bank projects in Africa. Eventually, the World Bank hopes to make this resource available to other stakeholders such as African governments and donor agencies (World Bank 2011).

African Diaspora Investment Fund (ADIF):

This initiative is the result of discussions with the International Finance Corporation (IFC) regarding a collaboration between the African Development Bank (AfDB), the African Regional Economic Communities (RECs), donor partners, diaspora members and other stakeholders to establish an investment fund for African diaspora members across the globe. The objective is to establish an offshore fund that would create multi-class shares denominated in multi-currencies.

The World Bank has not yet confirmed details such as the

fund's objectives and business targets and who will be responsible for its management (World Bank 2011).

Development Marketplace for the African Diaspora in Europe (DMADE):

DMADE Launched in 2007, this program utilized bilateral grants from Belgium, Germany, France and the Netherlands to make $1 million available to European-based African diaspora entrepreneurs who had proposals for sustainable businesses. Of the 500 business proposals received, 16 were chosen to receive funding. The winning proposals included a business to produce high-end textiles in Mali and another to process cashew nuts in the Ivory Coast (World Bank 2011). The deadline for applications closed in 2008. The World Bank has not published whether there will be a second round of this program.

Ethiopian Diaspora Health and Education Professionals Mobilization Project:

Funded by the Italian Government, this initiative will extend a pilot program that enables qualified members of the Ethiopian Diaspora to help build the capacity of Addis Ababa University through virtual volunteering.

Support for African diaspora networks:

Through the African Diaspora Program, the World Bank has provided support to several organizations managed by and for African diaspora members in the United States. These include the African Union-African Diaspora Health Initiative, implemented by the African Union Representational Mission to the United States.

Eligibility: Eligibility for World Bank programs and resources varies depending on the desires of the institutions funding the program.

Members of diasporas from any country within the African Union and living in any region of the world will be eligible to apply for the DMADA program through a legally registered organization. The African Diaspora skills database is open to all diaspora professionals interested in getting involved with their countries of origin.

Getting Involved: Aside from the African Diaspora Professional Skills Database, the initiatives described above are either in process or no longer active. To register in the database, diaspora professionals can submit a Basic Information Form and CV or corporate profile to afrdiaspora@worldbank.org. One World Bank publication claims that a link to the Basic Information Form can be found on the ADP homepage; however, I found that it was slightly more hidden. To access this form, diaspora members can go to the ADP website and click on the link under the News and Events Section entitled "World Bank African Diaspora Program Launches Database of Professional Skills." A link to the Basic Information Form can be found in the last paragraph on this webpage. For individuals interested in getting involved with the DMADA and/or ADIF programs, updates on the progress of these programs should be posted on the ADP's website as they occur.

RECOMMENDATIONS AND CONCLUSIONS

Efforts that combine the resources and technical expertise of traditional development actors with the knowledge and deeply held personal motivations of diaspora associations and individuals have enormous potential to improve the health and well being of home communities. But to date, very few of the varied organizations and programs seeking to support diaspora development work have withstood the test of time, and some are so new that they have yet to be evaluated.

There are also many factors that hinder this collaborative potential. Simply locating necessary information about potential partnerships can be extremely challenging, due in part to the vagaries of the internet and website formation. The integrity and effectiveness of these partnerships is also threatened by the often unequal balance of power between diaspora organizations and the traditional development actors. We therefore conclude this guide with a few practical suggestions for those in the diaspora seeking to locate and access resources, as well as for organizations that aim to form productive, co-development, solidarity-oriented partnerships.

General Suggestions for Diaspora Members and Organizations

Advocate for your needs: The most promising programs aimed at reinforcing the efforts of diaspora development actors were established at the request of diaspora members themselves. These include the Diaspora Volunteering Program in the UK, which DFID funded in response to lobbying by VSO and DVA. In the case of French co-development policies, criticism voiced by the African diaspora in France resulted in the reformation of these programs to reduce their emphasis on return migration (Panizzon 2011). Given current trends toward leveraging migration for development, organizations may be particularly responsive to the requests of diaspora members. Some countries and organizations have created formal networking platforms for this purpose, where diaspora members can interface with other organizations, public institutions, and policymakers. For diaspora members who don't have access to such a resource, spontaneously created diaspora networks have also made significant gains leveraging resources for programs that reflect their needs and priorities. For example, UK-based AFFORD has exerted significant influence over DFID, including lobbying them to create Connections for Development (de Haas 2006).

Search web platforms that offer clearinghouses and advertise multiple programs and opportunities: Aside from the organizations devoted entirely to working with diaspora members and organizations, most of the organizations supporting diaspora development work implement programs that are active for relatively short periods of time. This can complicate the process of locating resources because windows of opportunity are often of small duration and, after programs close, it is generally unclear whether additional opportunities will follow. Even while programs are active, they may not be open to new participants. For these reasons, websites that advertise opportunities and deadlines from multiple organizations are very valuable. The websites for FORIM, Connections for Development, DVA, FORIM, IdEA, and MyWorld all provide information on news and events that are relevant to diaspora development actors. These include funding opportunities and deadlines, workshops and trainings, volunteer opportunities, jobs in international development, and other useful resources.

Be persistent when trying to contact organizations. Regardless of the size of the organization, it can take multiple phone calls or emails, or both, to receive a response. Many organizations simply do not have the capacity to respond to every request and it is often the more persistent people who succeed in getting responses.

Suggestions for diaspora organizations seeking resources for development projects or capacity building

Start Small: Particularly for less-established diaspora organizations, it is a good idea to first seek support from smaller organizations that work exclusively with diaspora communities. These organizations are more likely to work with diaspora organizations with varied levels of experience and professionalization. They also have greater capacity to offer more individualized attention to help diaspora organizations locate and access appropriate resources. In contrast, larger organizations typically offer capacity building resources or technical assistance to organizations that have proven track records or with whom they already partner. Examples of organizations that offer training, workshops, and technical assistance to diaspora members and organizations include FORIM, CfD, ERCMOVE, DVA and IntEnt.

Build partnerships with other organizations: Most funding agencies and organizations either encourage or require diaspora organizations to implement projects in partnership with local organizations in the communities they seek to impact. This way, both organizations can benefit from sharing resources and expertise. Diaspora organizations that can demonstrate a history of building successful partnerships with other organizations also have more credibility when applying for grants from larger organizations like national development agencies.

For diaspora members who wish to contribute their skills:

Volunteering can be a highly rewarding and effective way for diaspora members to give back to and connect with their countries of origin. VSO has voiced the desire to pursue programs that mobilize diaspora youth, but most programs focus on mobilizing skilled and highly educated professionals.

Diaspora members seeking out opportunities may find it difficult to find assignments that match their skills, availability, and intended destination, as most organizations have programs that are active intermittently and in very particular countries. Recognizing this issue, IdEA is in the process of creating an online resource that will allow diaspora members to search for appropriate programs from a database of organizations involved in diaspora volunteering, but it is not yet available. Mainstream volunteering programs often recruit volunteers continually and have a sustained presence in far more countries than programs exclusively for diaspora volunteers. As diaspora members have felt excluded from mainstream volunteer programs in the past, VSO is working to adapt their programs to be more responsive to the needs of diaspora volunteers. Other organizations potentially willing to be flexible for diaspora volunteers include USAID's Volunteers for Prosperity.

Register in databases: the IOM's MIDA, the World Bank, the UNDP's TOKTEN, and FORIM, all possess databases in which diaspora professionals can advertise their skills. These are generally used by the organizations themselves, as well as African governments and institutions, to mobilize diaspora members when appropriate opportunities arise.

For remitting diaspora members and organizations:

Diaspora members are always on the look out for less costly and more efficient ways to send money home. Aid agencies, multilateral actors, and private entities such as banks, are all working to improve these transfers. There are also less savory actors seeking only to profit from this market. Arguably, some of the most effective tools for this purpose are websites like the

(originally sendmoneyhome.org) that allow diaspora members to compare services to find the fastest and least expensive way to transfer money. IntEnt (www.geldnaarhuis.nl) and the French government.

(www.envoidargent.fr) have developed similar comparison services. With many organizations engaged in efforts to increase the security, effectiveness, and scope of these services, it is hopeful that they will become accessible to more individuals sending and receiving remittances throughout the globe.

Other organizations seek to harness remittances for development by creating ways to channel funds into sustainable, productive investments. France offers co-development savings accounts that provide owners with tax deductions of almost 40% of the account's entire value when they invest in pre-defined infrastructure projects (Panizzon 2011). Other initiatives include AFFORD's RemitPlus campaign, which advocates for tax breaks on remittances spent in ways that further the MDGs. These tax breaks would be pooled into a fund that could be used to improve the creditworthiness of developing countries and to introduce social enterprises into the remittance transfer sector (AFFORD 2012).

For diaspora members who wish to start enterprises in their countries of origin:

In contrast, organizations like IntEnt and the SEVA Network in the Netherlands have been quite successful at equipping diaspora members at all levels of experience with the skills and resources needed to start successful businesses. These programs provide entrepreneurs with training, technical assistance, and, in the case of the Seva Network, start-up loans and grants to help diaspora entrepreneurs turn their business ideas into fully functional enterprises. While IntEnt does not supply entrepreneurs with funding, they provide assistance that is shown to be effective in connecting entrepreneurs with resources from outside sources. Not everyone who begins the program starts a business, but the businesses that are established have a very high success rate (Newland, Tanaka 2010). AFFORD also partners with IntEnt to provide enterprise development services for UK-based diaspora members wishing to start enterprises in Ghana.

Suggestions for traditional agents of development:

Improve interface with diaspora communities:

For diaspora development actors, finding and accessing appropriate resources can be an immensely challenging process. While conducting research for this guide, we found that necessary information about getting involved and accessing resources was scattered, difficult to find, or nonexistent on many organization's websites. As the chapters in "Done Waiting" reveal, the highly effective diaspora development actors that seek out these resources are frequently full-time workers who devote almost all of their spare time to development solidarity. Increasing the accessibility of information about getting involved would ensure that diaspora members are able to spend more time giving back to their communities, and, for traditional development actors, would likely reduce the amount of time spent fielding calls and emails about programs.

In the long term, it would be immensely helpful if practitioners working in the field of migration and development came together to create an online, international database of resources for diaspora development actors. Given that there are limited windows of opportunity to take advantage of many resources and strict eligibility requirements make many programs open only to diaspora members with very particular host and home countries, a database offering diaspora members a way to search for resources that match their particular qualifications and objectives would be immensely helpful.

Though particular to the Netherlands, the website myworld.nl provides an excellent example of how web platforms can be used to make the development world more accessible to diaspora organizations and other grass roots development actors.

Learn from the experiences of others:

Just because migration and development is a relatively new field does not mean that all programs need to be experimental. The Netherlands and France have decades of experience, both good and bad, that organizations and countries new to migration and development work can learn from. Many organizations emphasize innovation at the expense of continuing to implement and refine methods that have already achieved success. Proven engagement mechanisms like the Diaspora Volunteering Program and IntEnt, which have the potential benefit diaspora development actors and their communities throughout the globe, are limited to single countries. Combining experimental programs with those that are already proven could help ensure that diaspora members have access to resources that are more consistently effective. From this solid base, organizations could revise and innovate to adjust to the needs of particular contexts.

Build upon existing diaspora initiatives:

As this volume has sought to show, migrants help democratize development when they share their first-hand knowledge of local context, their in-country networks, and their deep personal motivations for improving the well being of those they left behind. Based upon diaspora members' unique histories, experiences, and sources of knowledge, their members' priorities, attitudes, and methods often differ from those of traditional development agent. As communities in developing countries have infinitely diverse needs, the world stands to benefit from an approach to development that encompasses a myriad of voices and methods. According to de Haas, "the challenge for development agencies is not to make diaspora organizations more like them but to work with them to build on their unique strengths and minimize their limitations" (de Haas 2006). The current focus, however, is on diaspora organizations adapting to mainstream development, rather than the other way around (Talbot 2011). For example, the eligibility requirements for many funding programs ask that potential diaspora partners conform to the priorities and methods of the funding partner. As diaspora organizations and traditional agents of development alike have much to gain through mutual learning, efforts should be made to minimize power imbalances and top-down decision making models. This would allow for greater flexibility and innovation to respond to the specific needs of recipient communities.

Bottom-up approaches to equipping diaspora development also have the potential to be more effective because they engender a greater sense of ownership and often have more credibility among diaspora communities. Studies on diaspora engagement identify stakeholder ownership as an important condition for success (de Haas 2006). The Diaspora Volunteering Program, which empowered diaspora organizations to implement their own volunteer programs, provides a good example of a more bottom-up approach. Partly as a result, many of these programs are on their way to being self-sustaining.

Final Thoughts

Collaboration between diaspora communities and traditional development actors that is based upon mutual respect and shared learning has immense potential to remedy many of the problems that have long plagued top-down, dependency creating, and unsustainable forms of development. At their best, such collaborations can build upon the already impressive works diaspora members have begun throughout the world. Powerful synergies can be created when the knowledge, experience, and unique strengths of the African diaspora are paired with the resources and know-how of traditional development agents. We hope that diaspora organizations and traditional development agents alike will use this guide to realize potential of such partnerships in order to achieve a common vision for a more equitable world.

ADDITIONAL SOURCES OF SUPPORT

To limit this guide to 25 profiles, we excluded many organizations that are potentially valuable resources to diaspora development actors. These include organizations that focus primarily on generating research, organizations doing work similar to those we had already decided to profile, and organizations that do not explicitly support diaspora development work. Here, you will find a list of these organizations and a short summary of their activities and objectives.

African Diaspora Policy Centre (ADPC), the Hague-the Netherlands, diaspora-centre.org: Generates research, formulates policy recommendations, and organizes networking events to increase the involvement and influence of the African Diaspora in international development. They are also an implementing partner for the Africa-Europe Platform for Development.

Africa Rural Connect, Web-based Platform, arc.peacecorpsconnect.org: Program implemented by the National Peace Corps Association that seeks to unite stakeholders in Africa's development (African Diaspora members, returned Peace Corps volunteers, development workers, farmers, etc.) to address challenges facing rural Africa. Members can post ideas for projects, comment on or endorse the ideas of others, and collaborate to turn ideas into concrete actions. Periodic contests provide cash prizes to the best proposals.

Africa UK, London-United Kingdom, africa-uk.org: Platform to promote research and networking to increase involvement of UK-based African Diaspora members in policymaking and international development.

Aga Khan Foundation, International, akdn.org: Foundation that supports grassroots organizations with ideas to create sustainable change in the areas of health, education, rural development, the environment, and strengthening civil society.

American International Health Alliance HIV/AIDS Twinning Center, Washington D.C.-United States, twinningagainstaids.org: Government-sponsored program that facilitates partnerships between American and African institutions for the treatment and prevention of aids. They run a volunteer program recruits healthcare workers in the African Diaspora to volunteer in hospitals and clinics in 11 Sub-Saharan African countries.

Centro Studi di Politica Internazionale (CeSPI), Rome-Italy, cespi.it: Source of research about topics related to international development and politics, including migration and development. Implementing partner for COOPI to equip diaspora efforts of Senegalese migrants.

Centro de Informação e Documentação Anti-Colonial (CIDAC), Lisbon-Portugal, cidac.pt: Generates research to promote the positive links between migration and development and partners with CfD to implement IDEM.

Coca-Cola Foundation, International, http://www.thecocacolacompany.com/citizenship/foundation_coke.html:

Provides financial support for community-based projects that focus on water stewardship, community recycling, healthy lifestyles, education, HIV/AIDS and malaria prevention, and job

creation. They also provides a donation-matching program for Coca-Cola employees.

Coordination Générale des Migrants pour le Développement (CGMD), Brussels-Belgium, cgmd.be: National organization similar to FORIM that encourages and facilitates research, networking, and awareness raising to strengthen and promote the influence and actions of diaspora organizations in Belgium. Implementing partner for the Africa-Europe Platform for Development.

Cooperazione per lo Sviluppo dei Paesi Emergenti (COSPE), Florence-Italy, cospe.it: International development organization that works to promote the rights of migrants.

Cuso International, Ottawa-Canada, cusointernational.org: Partners with VSO to provide professionals in North America with opportunities to volunteer abroad. They value the development contributions of diaspora members and implement diaspora volunteering programs in Ethiopia, Guyana, and Rwanda. Also partner with IdEA to implement their Diaspora Volunteering Program.

CCFD-Terre Solidaire (CCFD), Paris-France, ccfdterre-solidaire.org: Development NGO that conducts activities primarily by providing funding to other organizations. They are active in promoting the rights and development activities of

diaspora groups in France, one of pS-Eau's funding partners.

Global Forum for Migration and Development, International, gfmd.org: An annual meeting that convenes policy makers, high-level practitioners, and other stakeholders from UN member states to discuss policies, challenges, opportunities, and best practices in migration and development. Their website is a good source of information about national migration and development policies

Here and Home, Riverside, CA-United States, hereandhome.org: Nonprofit founded by African college and university faculty members in the US. They support higher education in Africa by recruiting academics in the African diaspora to teach summer courses or professional development workshops in African universities.

International Executive Service Corps (IESC), Washington, D.C.-United States, iesc.org: Mobilizes business and technological expertise in America to promote sustainable development. They recruit diaspora members for programs in Ethiopia, Lebanon, and Sudan.

International Labor Organization (ILO), International, ilo.org: UN organization that works to promote social justice by encouraging decent employment opportunities and protecting workers rights. Involved in implementing the UN-EU Joint Migration and Development Initiative.

SEVA Network Foundation: the Hague-the Netherlands, seva-group.org: Diaspora-led organization that seeks to reduce poverty by promoting entrepreneurship among Diaspora members and organizations. Provide financial support, technical assistance, and networking opportunities to Diaspora entrepreneurs.

The African Network (TAN), Santa Clara, CA-United States, the Africannetwork.org: Nonprofit organization that supports entrepreneurship among people of African descent. Organizes monthly networking dinners, an annual conference for African professionals, and events to train, encourage, and equip start-up entrepreneurs in underserved communities in Africa.

Veolia Environment Foundation, France, foundation.veolia.com: Corporate foundation committed to promoting community-oriented projects that contribute to outreach, workforce development, and environmental conservation. Previously supported an initiative of a Cameroonian Diaspora organization in France.

Volunteers for Economic Growth Alliance (VEGA), Washington D.C-United States, vegaalliance.org: Nonprofit committed to supporting emerging economies by mobilizing expertise and providing technical assistance.

APPENDIX D.

Informational Papers: What We Know About Diasporas and Economic Development

By <u>Kathleen Newland</u> and <u>Sonia Plaza</u>

Diasporas can play an important role in the economic development of their countries of origin. Beyond their well-known role as senders of remittances, diasporas can also promote trade and foreign direct investment, create businesses and spur entrepreneurship, and transfer new knowledge and skills. Although some policymakers see their nationals abroad as a loss, they are increasingly realizing that an engaged diaspora can be an asset — or even a counterweight to the emigration of skilled and talented migrants.

The impact of diaspora engagement is difficult to assess, due to the difficulty disentangling causation and correlation, and quantifying the impact of elusive goods like skills and knowledge transfers. However, we do know that governments can certainly do more to remove obstacles and create opportunities for diasporas to engage in economic development. Specific actions include identifying goals, mapping diaspora location and skills, fostering a relationship of trust with the diaspora, maintaining sophisticated means of communication with the diaspora, and ultimately encouraging diaspora contributions to national development.

Governmental diaspora-focused entities in countries of origin need to play a dual role, both facilitating diaspora contributions to the homeland, and serving the diaspora.

MEDIA RESOURCES Contact

Michelle Mittelstadt
202-266-1910
mmittelstadt@migrationpolicy.org

Diasporas Matter to development

The backbone of Diaspora contributions to global prosperity come in the form of remittances – the financial resources sent back to their countries of origin. In 2013, global remittances were estimated to be $550 billion, an amount over sixteen times U.S. official development assistance. The result of these resilient contributions often exceeds their monetary value. The flow of remittances allows parents to afford a child's school fees, supports entrepreneurs to open businesses, or helps families to buy food during economic shocks.

As Diaspora populations grow in the U.S. and internationally, so have the scope of their contributions beyond individual remittances.

- Diasporas Innovate– Diaspora entrepreneurs and scientists are creating innovations and growing the U.S. economy. Immigrant-owned businesses generated an estimated $67 billion in U.S. business income in 2011. Abroad, Diaspora entrepreneurs are also gearing investments toward their countries of origin.
- Diasporan scientists have long been among the most

influential innovators and change makers in their countries of origin.

- <u>Diasporas Give Back</u> – Diasporas often have the connections, linguistic and cultural competence, knowledge, and drive to serve as volunteers worldwide. There are 200,000 first- and second-generation immigrants among the 1 million U.S. residents who spend time volunteering abroad each year.
- Diasporas Invest – In the U.S. and abroad, Diasporas are creating greater economic opportunities. Diaspora investors in the U.S. from India, Mexico, Ghana and elsewhere are providing much needed capital to home economies through various financial instruments.
- Diasporas are Engaged – Today, Diasporas are making significant contributions to their ancestral homes. USAID's Diaspora Networks Alliance (DNA) framework guides its work with diaspora communities to promote economic and social growth in multiple countries.

Partnerships in Action

In recognition of the historic and growing influence of Diasporas on global development, USAID partners with Diaspora philanthropic and volunteer groups, investors, entrepreneurs and innovators to support and strengthen its assistance efforts abroad. USAID leverages these partnerships even further by working with donors, foundations, and corporations that support diaspora engagement.

To unleash the potential of diaspora engagement, USAID in collaboration with the State Department created the International diaspora Engagement Alliance (IdEA). IdEA harnesses the global connections of diaspora communities to promote sustainable development in their countries of origin.

USAID also works with Diaspora through a wide range of partnership initiatives that include:

- The Diasporas for Development Initiative, a partnership with Accenture and Cuso International to encourage diaspora volunteerism by recruiting highly-skilled diaspora professionals to support local development projects in select countries.
- Fostering scientific innovation and collaboration in developing countries through the Partnership for Enhanced Engagement in Research (PEER) program.

ABOUT THE AUTHOR

Dr. Michael Ralph, has recently served as a Southern University System Assistant Vice President and later, interim Vice President. Currently he is CEO and President of College & University Professional Accreditation Services, CUPAS. In his current role he assumes the leadership for CUPAS while serving as an accreditation expert and consultant to his business partners and their college and university clients throughout the United States. He is a consultant in higher education leadership, administration, accreditation, strategic planning and a frequent panelist and keynote speaker at professional conferences and meetings. Dr. Ralph is a New York University Scholar in leadership, administration, and strategic planning, with an earned doctorate in higher education from New York University, USA. He also has a Masters Degree in International Relations and Political Science from the University of British Columbia, Canada.

Michael is the proud husband of Lynette Ralph and father of their three wonderful and accomplished sons. In his spare time he enjoys book and poetry authorship, traveling music and quiet meditation. He considers himself deeply spiritual and believes in the mind and body connection and the interdependence and universality of all living things. He enjoys volunteering and serving the less fortunate and other worthy causes. Books published by Dr. Ralph are:

© 2016, The FUN Blueprint for Diaspora Engagement,

© 2016, The Indisputable Resilience of Arch: A Guyanese – American

© 2015, A Riddle, A Mystery, An Enigma and a Conundrum: Sunderland University

© 2009, Voices I. Voices in Tribute to President Barack Obama, Our Nation's 44th President

© 2001, Empowering Choices! Infinite Possibilities.

For additional information see: Main website: www.ralphbooks.com & Facebook Link to: www.bitly.com/drmichaelralphsr

UNCOMMON SENSE;

ADDRESSED TO THE

CITIZENS

OF

AMERICA,

On the following important

SUBJECTS:

"If men cannot save themselves by common sense, they cannot save each other by coercion." – G. K. Chesterton

J. M. PAYNE

DEDICATION:

To my Father, who taught me to use my mind;
To my Mother, who taught me about the heart;
To Lindita, who has always been at my side;
& to Peri Parks, author of "Reset: A Thriller",
who bravely undertook the task of editing:

THANK YOU.

FOR ANY PARTICULAR SUBJECT:
"One percent of people Think;
Nine percent think that they Think;
Ninety percent would rather die than Think.
The one percent cause most of the progress;
The nine percent cause most of the problems; &
The ninety percent don't cause much of anything.
Be one of the one percent."
James T. Payne, Sr
My father

"The most powerful motivation to Think
Is to have control over one's own affairs;
This is why Liberty works."
Jeffrey M. Payne
His son